STANLEY K. STOWERS is Assistant
Professor, Department of Religious
Studies, Brown University.

Letter Writing
in Greco-Roman Antiquity

Library of Early Christianity

Wayne A. Meeks, General Editor

Letter Writing
in Greco-Roman Antiquity

Stanley K. Stowers

The Westminster Press
Philadelphia

© 1986 Stanley K. Stowers

Scripture quotations from the Revised Standard Version of the Bible are copyrighted 1946, 1952, © 1971, 1973 by the Division of Christian Education of the National Council of the Churches of Christ in the U.S.A. and are used by permission.

Book design by Gene Harris

First edition

Published by The Westminster Press®
Philadelphia, Pennsylvania

PRINTED IN THE UNITED STATES OF AMERICA

9 8 7 6 5 4 3 2 1

Library of Congress Cataloging-in-Publication Data

Stowers, Stanley Kent.
    Letter writing in Greco-Roman antiquity.

    (Library of early Christianity ; 5)
    Bibliography: p.
    Includes index.
    1. Classical letters—History and criticism.
2. Letter-writing, Classical. 3. Bible. N.T.
Epistles—Language, style. 4. Fathers of the church.
5. Church history—Primitive and early church, ca. 30–600.
6. Civilization, Greco-Roman. I. Title. II. Series.
PA3042.S86 1986   886'.01'09   86–9082
ISBN 0-664-21909-8

I dedicate this book to the memory of Horst Moehring, mentor, colleague, and friend—who created the graduate program in which I have been privileged to teach and learn so much.

Contents

Foreword

This series of books is an exercise in taking down fences. For many years the study of ancient Christianity, and especially of the New Testament, has suffered from isolation, but happily that situation is changing. For a variety of reasons, we have begun to see a convergence of interests and, in some instances, real collaboration by scholars across several academic boundaries: between Roman historians and historians of Christianity, between New Testament scholars and church historians, between historians of Judaism and of Christianity, between historical and literary scholars.

The Library of Early Christianity harvests the fruit of such collaboration, in several areas in which fresh approaches have changed the prevailing view of what the early Christians were like. Much of what is presented here has not been brought together in this fashion before. In order to make this information as accessible as possible, we have not burdened the books with the sort of argument and documentation that is necessary in scholarly monographs, in which such new work is ordinarily presented. On the other hand, the authors do not condescend to their readers. Students in colleges and seminaries and at more advanced levels will find in these books an opportunity to participate in a conversation at the growing edge of current scholarship.

The common perspective of the series is that of social history. Both words of the phrase are equally important. The objects of study are the living Christian communities of the early centuries in their whole environment: not just their ideas, not only their leaders and heroes. And the aim is to understand those communities as they believed, thought, and acted then and there—not to "explain" them by some supposedly universal laws of social behavior.

The study of early Christian letters within the context of ancient epistolography has made rapid advances in recent years. Even so, the focus of many investigations has been very narrow, inquiring only about particular formal elements. Too often rigidly defined types of ancient letters have been made Procrustean beds into which actual letters were forced. The variety of functions that letters served has seldom received attention. In a direct and lively fashion, Stanley Stowers shows us the wide array of things that people did with letters in antiquity, the way ancient critics and teachers described these different functions, and concrete examples of many kinds and levels: from handbooks, from literary letters, from popular letters. And he has pointed out many specific ways this material can illuminate our study of the letters of the New Testament and all of early Christian correspondence.

WAYNE A. MEEKS
General Editor

Acknowledgments

I wish to thank Cynthia L. Thompson and Wayne A. Meeks for providing me with the opportunity to write a book that would attempt to locate early Christian letters within a broad cultural context. Their patient editorial assistance also deserves acknowledgment. I am grateful to Mary Alyce Gasbarro for her indispensable word-processing skills.

Unless otherwise specified, all translations of the handbooks under the names of Libanius (Proclus) and Demetrius are from Abraham J. Malherbe's "Ancient Epistolary Theorists," *(Ohio) Journal of Religious Studies* 5(1977), which I have abbreviated as AET. I have used Malherbe's translations with the permission of the *Journal of Religious Studies.*

I am grateful for permission to reprint copyrighted material from the following works:

Pseudo-Anacharsis, *Epistles,* trans. Anne M. McGuire, in *The Cynic Epistles,* ed. Abraham J. Malherbe. Missoula, Mont.: Scholars Press, 1977. Reprinted by permission of the publisher.

The Apostolic Fathers, II, trans. Kirsopp Lake. Cambridge, Mass.: Harvard University Press, 1913. Reprinted by permission of the Loeb Classical Library and the publisher.

Augustine, *Select Letters,* trans. J. H. Baxter. Cambridge, Mass.: Harvard University Press, 1930. Reprinted by permission of the Loeb Classical Library and the publishers.

Augustine, *Letters,* I, trans. Wilfred Parsons. New York: Fathers of the Church, 1953. Reprinted by permission of the publisher, The Catholic University of America Press.

Basil, *Letters,* I, II, IV, trans. Roy J. Deferrari. Cambridge, Mass.: Harvard University Press, 1926, 1928, 1934. Reprinted by permission of the Loeb Classical Library and the publishers.

Cicero, *Letters to His Friends,* I, II, III, trans. W. Glynn Williams. Cambridge, Mass.: Harvard University Press, 1927, 1929. Reprinted by permission of the Loeb Classical Library and the publishers.

Pseudo-Crates, *Epistles,* trans. Ronald Hock in *The Cynic Epistles,* ed. Abraham J. Malherbe. Missoula, Mont.: Scholars Press, 1977. Reprinted by permission of the publisher.

Pseudo-Demetrius, *On Style,* trans. W. Rhys Roberts. Cambridge, Mass.: Harvard University Press, 1932. Reprinted by permission of the publishers and the Loeb Classical Library.

Pseudo-Diogenes, *Epistles,* trans. Benjamin Fiore in *The Cynic Epistles,* ed. Abraham J. Malherbe. Missoula, Mont.: Scholars Press, 1977. Reprinted by permission of the publisher.

Epicurus, *Epicurus, the Extant Remains,* trans. Cyril Bailey. Oxford: Oxford University Press, 1926. Reprinted by permission of the publisher.

Fronto, *The Correspondence of Marcus Cornelius Fronto,* trans. C. R. Haines. Cambridge, Mass.: Harvard University Press, 1919, 1920. Reprinted by permission of the publishers and the Loeb Classical Library.

Julian, *Letters,* trans. W. C. Wright. Cambridge, Mass.: Harvard University Press, 1923. Reprinted by permission of the publishers and the Loeb Classical Library.

The Oxyrhynchus Papyri 42, ed. and trans. P. J. Parsons. London: Egypt Exploration Society, 1974. Reprinted by courtesy of the Egypt Exploration Society of London.

Philostratus, *Life of Apollonius of Tyana; Epistles of Apollonius,* trans. F. C. Conybeare. Cambridge, Mass.: Harvard University Press, 1912. Reprinted by permission of the publishers and the Loeb Classical Library.

Seneca, *Epistulae Morales,* trans. R. M. Gummere. Cambridge, Mass.: Harvard University Press, 1917, 1920, 1925. Reprinted by permission of the publishers and the Loeb Classical Library.

Pseudo-Socrates and the Socratics, *Epistles,* trans. Stanley K. Stowers, in *The Cynic Epistles,* ed. Abraham J. Malherbe. Missoula, Mont.: Scholars Press, 1977. Reprinted by permission of the publisher.

Abbreviations

AET	Abraham J. Malherbe, "Ancient Epistolary Theorists," *(Ohio) Journal of Religious Studies* 5(1977)
AJA	*American Journal of Archaeology*
AJPh	*American Journal of Philology*
BJRL	*Bulletin of the John Rylands Library*
Corp. Pap. Jud.	*Corpus Papyrorum Judaicarum*
JEA	*Journal of Egyptian Archaeology*
LCL	Loeb Classical Library
NDIEC	*New Documents Illustrating Early Christianity,* ed., tr., and annotated by G. H. R. Horsley (Ancient History Documentary Research Center, Macquarie University, 1981)
NPNF	*Nicene and Post-Nicene Fathers of the Christian Church,* ed. Philip Schaff, 1887–1894
OGIS	*Orientis Graeci Inscriptiones Selectae,* 1903–1905
P.Bon.	*Papyri Bononienses*
P.Grenf.	B. P. Grenfell and A. S. Hunt, *New Classical Fragments and Other Greek and Latin Papyri*
P.Harr.	*The Rendel Harris Papyri of Woodbrooke College, Birmingham*
P.Heidelb.	*Veröffentlichungen aus der Heidelberger Papyrussammlung*

P.Herm.	*Papyri from Hermopolis and Other Documents of the Byzantine Period*
P.Jews	*Jews and Christians in Egypt,* ed. H. I. Bell
P.Lond.	*Greek Papyri in the British Museum*
P.Merton	*A Descriptive Catalogue of the Greek Papyri in the Collection of Wilfred Merton*
P.Oxy.	*Oxyrhynchus Papyri*
P.Par.	*Notices et extraits des papyrus grecs du Musée du Louvre et de la Bibliothèque Impériale*
P.Teb.	*Tebtunis Papyri*
P.Wisc.	*Wisconsin Papyri*
PG	*Patrologia Graeca,* ed. J. P. Migne
PSI	*Papyri greci e latini* (Pubbl. della Società Italiana per la ricerca dei papiri greci e latini in Egitto)
SB	*Sammelbuch griechischer Urkunden aus Ägypten*
UPZ	*Urkunden der Ptolemäerzeit*
ZPE	*Zeitschrift für Papyrologie und Epigraphik*

PART ONE
Greco-Roman Letter Writing and Early Christianity

Something about the nature of early Christianity made it a movement of letter writers. We possess more than nine thousand letters written by Christians in antiquity. Twenty-one of the twenty-seven writings in the New Testament take the form of letters. Two of the remaining works, the Acts of the Apostles and the Apocalypse, contain letters within them. If the interpreter is willing to understand early Christian letters as Greco-Roman letters, they can provide a fascinating window into the world of those Christians.

From the modern perspective, it is natural to think about letters in terms of the information they communicate. The interpreter, however, should resist the temptation to overlook the great multiplicity of functions that letters performed and to speak only of the communication of information. It is more helpful to think of letters in terms of the actions that people performed by means of them. Consider, for example, the following things people could do with letters:

Order or request provisions
Elicit a virtue or promote a habit of behavior
Initiate a relationship with another person or group
Maintain a relationship with a person or group
End a relationship with a person or group
Restore a relationship with a person or group
Praise someone
Cause someone to be sorry
Give orders (a superior to a subordinate)
Give a report of events
Cause a group to share a common hope
Elicit capacities for social bonding
Threaten someone
Console someone

Mediate between individuals or groups about a certain matter
Give advice
Request advice
Express thanks
Give honor

The study of early Christian letters has suffered because the letters have too often been forced into an interpretive mold formed by two questions: What theology does it contain, and what ideas was the author trying to defend or attack? The foregoing list suggests the vast multiplicity of things people did by means of letters. The list also illustrates that ancient letters will be difficult to understand on their own terms unless we also understand something about the contexts of Greco-Roman society in which the actions were performed and had their meanings. Rebuking and giving praise and honor, for example, were very important activities in ancient letter writing and had a significance for Greco-Roman society that is without parallel in modern Western societies. Thus it is helpful for the interpreter of the New Testament and other contemporary letters to know something about the meanings, conventions, and institutions associated with honor and praise in the early Roman empire.

1

The Modern Study
of Early Christian Letters

A long succession of scholars have immensely enriched our understanding of early Christian letters. Perhaps the dominant figure is still Adolf Deissmann, whose writings before World War I have had a profound impact on New Testament scholarship. Deissmann was a pioneer in the study of the newly discovered papyri from Egypt. Until the discovery of the papyri from the trash heaps and archives of sand-covered towns, scholars had only inscriptions and documents preserved by literary transmission from which to form a picture of everyday life in antiquity. The papyri consisted mostly of writings not deemed worthy of literary preservation: contracts, wills, business and familial letters, receipts, tax lists. They have revealed much about everyday life that is missing from the literary sources.

Deissmann believed that the nonliterary papyrus letters from Egypt shed light on New Testament letters in three areas: the style and genre of the letters, the social class and context of the letter writers, and the relationship of Christian writings to Hellenistic and Jewish cultures. In contrast to later research, which has tended to focus on the form of the letters in isolation from questions of social context, Deissmann saw that literary form and social context were interrelated. Before Deissmann, scholars had tried to compare the New Testament literature to classical standards of literary style such as the works of Plato and Demosthenes. Some had even argued that it would be an aspersion against the Holy Spirit to say that the New Testament was written in anything but the best literary style.

Deissmann and his contemporaries showed that most of the New Testament writings were in many ways closer to the language of the common papyri than to Plato and Demosthenes. Deissmann, however, went much further than this in trying to specify the genre of the New Testament letters. He distinguished letters (or "real letters") from epistles ("non-real letters"). He said that letters are exemplified by the common business and familial papyrus letters. Letters are private, unliterary, purely occasional, and artless and merely convey information, like a telephone call today. Epistles are exemplified by the literary letters—not real letters at all—of writers such as Epicurus, Seneca, and Pliny; they are public (meant for publication or a wider audience), literary, conventional, and artful and are written for posterity. Letters are warm and personal; epistles are cold and impersonal.

According to Deissmann, the letters of Paul were clearly real letters and not epistles, works of literature. Deissmann painted a romantic picture of Paul, a champion of the lower classes and the uneducated, pouring forth his passionate responses to church crises in a way unaffected by literary or rhetorical convention. Deissmann introduced the idea that spontaneity was a characteristic of the ancient letter. In contrast, he classed James, 1 and 2 Peter, and Jude as epistles.

For Deissmann the papyri showed that early Christianity was a people's movement of the lower classes. It also demonstrated that the peculiar language and style of the New Testament writings were not due to Christianity's roots in Jewish culture, as many had argued. The language of the New Testament was not Semitic but common (i.e., Koine) Greek. Much of Deissmann's vividly illustrated portrait of early Christian letter writing has withstood the test of time, although not without important modification.

Deissmann was criticized almost immediately by a number of scholars for his letter–epistle distinction and for exaggerating the similarities of Paul's letters to the papyri. Nevertheless, New Testament scholars have found it very difficult to transcend Deissmann's two divisions: "real" and "nonreal" letters are still the most important genre categories in use. Deissmann's approach has also been perpetuated simply because most of the comparative study of New Testament letters has continued to be with the nonliterary (or documentary) papyri. Thus the relationship of the early Christian letters to the larger world of Greco-Roman letter writing, literature, and rhetoric is today a neglected and a pressing question. This is not just a question of form but also a question of how to understand the functions of early Christian letters in their original social and historical contexts. To what categories did early Christian letters belong? In what ways and contexts did they fulfill their functions?

It will be helpful to understand certain limitations of the Deissmann approach. First, it is now clear that the nonliterary papyrus letters from Egypt provide only a partial although important view of Greco-Roman letter writing. The papyri show us the life and culture of some small provincial towns in Egypt. In certain respects these towns were rather remote from the life of the great centers of Hellenistic culture such as the cities of Paul. If we could examine the papyrus remains of a trash heap or private archive from Ephesus or Corinth, we would probably see a somewhat different and much more complex picture of ancient epistolography. Therefore, it is of the utmost importance to include the evidence of letters preserved by literary transmission when we study early Christian letters. It is also essential to study theoretical statements made by ancient authors about letter writing and to study letters that were put forth as models for imitation.

Second, the distinction between private (letters) and public (epistles) does not hold well for either Greco-Roman society in general or for letter writing. Politics, for example, was based on the institutions of friendship and family. It is characteristic for moderns to think of politics as the epitome of the public sphere in contrast to friendship and family, which constitute the private sphere. The distinction between private friendly letters and public political letters is thus a distinction more appropriate to modernity than antiquity. Furthermore, many correspondences in antiquity that were either originally written or later edited with an eye toward publication have what we would call a private character: for example, Cicero, Ruricius, Seneca. It is difficult to answer the question, How public or private were Paul's letters? They were addressed to specific communities based in households, were meant to be read to any who were in attendance at the community assembly, and were perhaps copied and circulated to communities in other cities even before Paul's death. The distinction between private and public letters is not very helpful.

Third, the distinction between warm, personal, spontaneous, artless, common-private-friendly letters and impersonal, conventional, artificial literary letters is extremely misleading. Deissmann's antithesis between the natural and the conventional was typical of nineteenth- and early twentieth-century Romanticism popularized in Deissmann's day by the writings of Leo Tolstoy and others. Now, however, theorists of literature and culture are widely agreed that there is a conventional dimension to all intelligible human behavior. Thus Deissmann's dictum that "the letter is a piece of life, the epistle is a product of literary art" (*Light from the Ancient East*, p. 230) is a misguided contrast. All letters are literature in the very broadest sense. Even the common papyrus letters follow highly stylized letter-writing conventions. Literature in the narrow sense comes about because cultures, subcultures, and elite social classes draw boundaries and set standards that define aesthetic taste and literary artistry. Such standards, however, are specific to various societies. The historian should not fall into the trap of adopting the standards of any one time or place in such a way as to cause blindness to the broader literary culture of a society.

Therefore we must be very careful about distinctions between literary and nonliterary letters, real and nonreal letters, and genuine and pseudonymous letters. These have some validity but should not be used to define the letter so narrowly that we miss the larger phenomenon of what people actually did with letters in antiquity.

Since Deissmann wrote, researchers have made important refinements in understanding the literary conventions that open and close letters. We owe the greatest advances in the understanding of New Testament letters to those who have worked in this area. This is especially true for the Pauline letters. Scholars have focused their attention on them. This emphasis on Paul has sometimes had the unfortunate consequence that other New Testament and early Christian letters are either considered less than genuine or are dismissed as derivative of Paul's letter form. Pseudonymous letters were important in early Christianity but scholars have neglected their study, both because of the narrow definition of the "real letter" and also because of the elevation of Paul's undisputedly authentic letters to the standard for earliest Christian epistolography.

Most extant Greek and Latin letters begin with a prescript or salutation that contains the name of the sender, the name of the addressee, and a greeting. The formula is: "Demetrius to Publius, greetings." This may be embellished and either abbreviated or expanded in various ways. Often the greeting was followed by a prayer for the recipient, sometimes by a wish for the recipient's health, and occasionally by a statement of thanksgiving to a god or gods. The letters usually end with the word "farewell." Sometimes the farewell is preceded by a wish for the health of the recipient or a request for the recipient to greet family members, friends, or others named by the sender.

These opening and closing formulas seem to have been of little interest to the ancients when they reflected on letter writing. Discussion of openings and closings is virtually absent from extant ancient epistolary theory, and in collections of letters, the opening and closing formulas are often abbreviated or omitted. Nevertheless, writers were clearly aware that variations on these formulas could be an important element in accomplishing the purposes of their letters. In the fictitious letter of Dionysius to Speusippus, the writer says, "I use 'Do well' in greeting you, if indeed it is better than 'Joy to you' (which it is not). But it is better than 'Have pleasure,' which Lasthenia and Speusippus use."[1] In a jesting vein the writer suggests that people can communicate their philosophy of life by the greeting they select.

Research on New Testament letters, especially the letters of Paul, has focused on showing how these Christian authors modified and adapted the typical opening and closing formulas for their own purposes. These modifications set the earliest Christian letters apart as the products of a unique religious community.

The common Hellenistic opening salutation, "A to B, greetings," is found in the letters in Acts 15:23 and 23:26, as well as James 1:1. Paul preserves one of the characteristics peculiar to Semitic letter writing when he adds a wish for peace to his greetings: "Grace to you and peace from God our Father and the Lord Jesus Christ" (Rom. 1:7; cf. Dan. 4:1). Since Paul's word "grace," *charis,* is related to the ordinary word "greeting," *chairein,* his salutation reads like a kind of Christian play on the standard formula. The word "grace" is important in Paul's thought and also may be a variation on "mercy" in the formula "peace and mercy" found in some Semitic letters. Paul and other early Christian writers turn the greeting into a wish for blessing from God. He elaborates on the name of the sender and the recipient and expands the greeting theologically. By this sort of modification, writers not only express Christian beliefs but also establish or confirm a particular religious relationship with their audience. Paul also clearly adapts his salutations so that they contribute to the particular purposes he hopes to accomplish in writing to a certain church. In the salutation to Romans, for example, he expands his name as sender into a summary of the gospel and a statement of his calling to be an apostle to the Gentiles (1:1–6). This anticipates the rest of the letter, where he introduces himself and his gospel for the Gentiles to the Christian communities at Rome.

A book by Paul Schubert, *The Form and Function of the Pauline Thanksgiving,* published in 1939, has shown how much can be learned from studying epistolary formulas. The inspiration of Schubert's book may explain the fixation of New Testament epistolary research on the openings and conclusions of Paul's letters. In the New Testament, only Pauline letters contain opening thanksgivings. They occur rarely in later Christian letters. The thanksgiving, however, is a genuine Hellenistic epistolary form that is seen occasionally in common papyrus letters.

Schubert argued that the thanksgiving was a characteristic feature of Paul's letters, which concluded the letter opening, suggested the purpose of the letter, and sometimes outlined its key topics. Later study has confirmed and refined Schubert's results. Paul mentions in his thanksgivings concerns he perceives to be important for the recipients of the letter. In 1 Corinthians (1:4–9), he gives thanks for the speech, knowledge, and spiritual gifts of the Corinthians. In chapters 1–4, 8, and 12–14 the reader learns that the improper uses of wisdom, knowledge, charismatic speech, and spiritual gifts are, according to Paul, central problems for the Corinthian church. Among Paul's letters, only Galatians lacks a thanksgiving. That absence is probably due to the nature of that letter. Paul is extremely upset with the Galatian community. Instead of a thanksgiving Paul uses another convention found in papyrus letters, an ironic rebuke. Thus he exclaims, "I am astonished that you are so quickly deserting the one who called you" (Gal. 1:6). The lack of his customary thanksgiving signals the mood and purpose of the letter. In 2 Corinthians the thanksgiving takes the form of a blessing with a liturgical sound to it. In fact, the thanksgiving is a kind of prayer.

Like many of the papyri and letters transmitted literarily, Paul's letters often close with greetings (Rom. 16:3–16; 1 Cor. 16:19–21; 2 Cor. 13:12–13; Phil. 4:21–22; 1 Thess. 5:26; Philemon 23–24). In Romans, 2 Corinthians, and 1 Thessalonians he exhorts, "Greet one another with a holy kiss." Instead of the common farewell, Paul employs a closing benediction, such as "The grace of our Lord Jesus Christ be with your spirit." Other non-papyrus Christian letters also frequently close with greetings and a benediction.

According to some scholars, the salutation and thanksgiving are followed by two other sections in the Pauline letter, the body and the paraenetic section—a text that strings together moral exhortations. Problems with these two divisions of the Pauline letter illustrate the limitations of the prevailing approach to earliest Christian letters. When Greek and Roman writers reflect on letter writing, they either discuss the "body" or consider the letter as a functioning whole. Modern epistolary research has found very little to say about the body of the letter. This major lacuna has occurred because scholars studying "epistolary" style have limited their analysis to elements thought to be unique to letters. Defined in that way, what is "epistolary" about letters shows up only at the beginnings and conclusions. Thus, the beginnings and endings of letters contain the true epistolary features, and what comes in between seems to be merely the information or message to be conveyed.

Ancient letter-writing theory, however, took a more holistic and functional approach. Letters were classified into types according to typical situations and social contexts of letter writing. This meant classification according to typical purposes that letter writers hoped to accomplish. The writer might wish to accuse someone of something, console a relative or friend, command a slave, or exhort someone to follow a certain way of life. From the ancient rhetorical perspective, verbal formulas, rhetorical figures, methods of argumentation, and so on could be used widely in various rhetorical genres. What differentiated a victory speech, a letter of congratulations, a judicial speech, and a discussion in the city council were the purposes to be accomplished in those particular contexts.

The letter is adaptable to a wide range of circumstances and purposes but always has the characteristic of being a "communication" between people who are separated. That makes the rhetoric of consoling someone or persuading someone to do something quite different than it would be if the person were present. Certain selections and combinations of linguistic formulas, rhetorical figures, methods of argumentation, and so on will generally be characteristic of certain types of letters. The work done by scholars on early Christian letters is extremely valuable but ought to be integrated into a less atomistic and more functional approach to letters. Above all, it is necessary to compare Christian letters to the whole range of letters and to approach them with a knowledge of ancient epistolary and rhetorical theory.

Scholars have understood paraenesis as the giving of miscellaneous moral precepts and exhortations. The idea that Paul's letters have paraenetic sections before their conclusions is not substantiated by the letters themselves and reflects a misunderstanding of what paraenesis is. Paraenesis has been understood too narrowly in New Testament studies. It is not just the stringing together of traditional precepts and exhortations. A whole paraenetic or hortatory tradition of rhetoric developed in antiquity. Paraenesis includes not only precepts but also such things as advice, supporting argumentation, various modes of encouragement and dissuasion, the use of examples, models of conduct, and so on. Abraham Malherbe has shown, for example, that 1 Thessalonians as a whole is a paraenetic letter that uses such rhetoric. It does not just have a paraenetic section after the thanksgiving and body of the letter. Romans is the letter of Paul that comes closest to having a discrete paraenetic section. Even with Romans, that division is misleading because the earlier part of the letter also contains hortatory materials.

Much fruitful work has been done on identifying and analyzing characteristic "forms" that occur between the opening and closing features. Again, most of this research has been on the letters of Paul and the Pauline school. These features include, for example, virtue and vice lists, apocalyptic statements, exhortations to households, autobiographical sections, Pauline travel plans, and hymns. Again, the next step in research ought to be an attempt to determine if these features have parallels in Greco-Roman epistolography which would suggest how they function in the larger rhetoric of letter types.

Research, for example, has shown that the opening materials of common papyrus letters were often followed by a request formula. One of the common expressions used in the papyri, Paul, and other Christian writers is *parakalō:* "I beseech" or "I exhort." Paul is said to be following the common papyrus request formula, as when someone writes, "I beseech you, please bring the wheat." But something has not been taken adequately into account. Not only common "letters of request" but also "paraenetic letters" use the formula. In the latter case, the expression is a type of exhortation and ought to be explained by ancient hortatory theory. In that tradition, *parakalō* has a long history as a semi-technical expression. Thus the same expressions may function differently in different types of letters. The larger perspective on the letter is essential. Recently there has been a revival of interest in the study of Greek and Roman rhetoric on the part of some New Testament scholars. A few classical scholars have also taken an interest in the New Testament and ancient rhetoric. Important beginnings have been made, beginnings that often take up the leads of scholars from the beginning of this century who were steeped in classical literature. It is too early, however, to speak of definitive results or widespread agreement among researchers.

The situation is quite different for research on literarily transmitted letters from the great age of Christian epistolography in the fourth and fifth centuries. These letters more easily lend themselves to analysis. Letter writers such as Basil, Gregory of Nyssa, Gregory of Nazianzus, Synesius, Ambrose, Jerome, and Augustine tend to follow the "textbooks" on rhetoric and epistolary theory. Furthermore, while scholars who work on the New Testament have sometimes proceeded as if the earliest Christians were not people of the Greco-Roman world, patristic scholars have always assumed that the church fathers had to be understood in that context. The remoteness of the later fathers from Judaism as compared to the New Testament authors and their higher educational level also make epistolographic research easier. Thus, to varying degrees, the letters of particular later patristic writers have been analyzed with regard to epistolary style, letter types, and rhetorical techniques.

The surviving letters from the second and third centuries (such as those of Ignatius and Cyprian) range between the New Testament letters and the later fathers in their conformity to the higher rhetorical standards. Most of these have not received adequate epistolographic study.

There is considerable variation among New Testament letters. But taken as a whole, they resemble neither the common papyri from the very lowest levels of culture and education nor the works of those with the highest levels of rhetorical training. They fall somewhere in between and have the cast of a Jewish subculture. Study of these letters in light of Greco-Roman epistolography can be an enormous aid to the exegesis and interpretation of the New Testament. When interpreters must rely solely on reconstructing a historical occasion for letters from clues within the letters themselves, they are caught in a vicious circle. The only basis for an interpretation of the letter is information derived from an interpretation of the letter. If, however, researchers can show through the comparative study of Greco-Roman letters that a New Testament letter follows or adapts certain conventions, is a certain type, or functions in a certain way, then the researcher has introduced an outside control over that vicious circle.

The possibilities for providing some interpretive determinacy will be best illustrated by an example from the New Testament. In 1 Thessalonians 2:1–12, Paul recounts the nature of his missionary work with the Thessalonians, giving a long list of antitheses. He says that his visit was not in vain but that he preached boldly with courage; his appeal did not spring from error, uncleanness, or guile but he spoke to please God; he did not flatter, preach for monetary gain, seek glory from men, or make harsh demands but he was gentle. Why did Paul write this list of antitheses about his preaching? How is one to understand what Paul is doing? A traditional approach has been to say that Paul sounds as if he is defending himself here against charges. It is reasoned that Paul was a controversial fellow who had many enemies. Paul had heard that some in this newly established community were accusing him of preaching in vain, being cowardly, preaching from error, uncleanness, and guile, attempting to please men as a flatterer, and being harsh. The passage is Paul's apology for his preaching. Throughout the letter, however, Paul indicates that his relationship with the Thessalonians is very good.

Abraham Malherbe has shown that 1 Thessalonians is packed with the characteristic features of a complex paraenetic letter. One often important feature of this kind of letter is the use of the author's own behavior as an example for imitation. At the same time, the writer, in good epistolary style, often reminds his readers of the basis of their friendship. This is exactly how 1 Thessalonians 2 functions. Paul reminds his readers of his founding work with them and thus illustrates his care and concern as their spiritual father. He also recalls their faithful reception of the gospel and their imitation of the Judean churches when under persecution. Later in the letter, he urges them to exhort and encourage one another, just as he had exhorted and encouraged them. Paul's behavior, then, becomes a model for their behavior toward one another. When one understands 1 Thessalonians as a paraenetic letter rather than a mirror, with a reverse image, it reads quite differently.

2

Letter Writing
and Greco-Roman Society

To understand early Christian letters more nearly as ancient writers and readers would have understood them requires some understanding of the typical social contexts of letter writing in the Greco-Roman world. Three sets of social relationships were central to that culture. First are hierarchical relations between subordinates and superordinates, best exemplified by the social institutions of the client-patron relationship. Second are relationships between equals epitomized by the Greek and Roman institutions of friendship. Third are the social relationships of the household, which combine characteristics of both hierarchical relations and relations between equals.

The giving of praise and blame was essential to the working of these institutions in antiquity. To praise meant to bestow honor; to blame meant to take away honor and cause shame. It was through honor that a person's rightful place in society was defined. Honor provided a person with a status in society. It was like a social rating that entitled the person to act and be treated in certain ways. People knew how to locate themselves and behave toward superiors, inferiors, and equals because of the system of honor.

Aristocrats inherited great honor from their family. They could often dispense honor to others. One could add to one's honor in certain ways: for instance, through feats of warfare or by attaining great wealth. In this type of society, honor exists when persons value themselves in a certain way and when that value is acknowledged by their social group. People in the society acknowledge another's honor by praising the person in a way that befits the person's role and status. A reproach or censure is a challenge to a person's claim to honor.

Most types of letters used in the Greco-Roman world were associated with the *epideictic* division of rhetoric. Following Aristotle, the ancients regarded epideictic as the rhetoric of praise and blame. Aristotle said that the purpose of epideictic was to honor or dishonor something or someone. Modern taste generally considers this type of rhetoric to be empty and useless. Expressions such as "It is mere rhetoric" reflect the typical modern evaluation. This attitude, however, betrays an acute failure to understand and appreciate how a different culture worked.

The Roman empire was fundamentally hierarchical.[2] It was a broad-based pyramid with slaves and free agricultural workers at the bottom and the emperor and Roman aristocracy at the top. This pyramid was replicated countless times on a smaller scale in all sorts of institutions and relationships. Religious groups, estates, workers guilds, and families were organized hierarchically. Access to power and security was only available through a relationship with someone who was socially superior. This is the client-patron relationship. Clients looked to aristocratic superiors who were supposed to exercise duties according to a code of liberality. Patrons interceded for clients and helped them in many ways. In return, the client, above all, owed the patron honor, an acknowledgment of the patron's social superiority. In this way, services and capital gifts were exchanged for honor expressed through praise and deferential behavior. Local aristocrats, for example, served as public officers for towns and provided finances for public works and services. In return, the towns honored the aristocrats by erecting statues and carving inscriptions in praise of them.

The writer of the following letter does nothing except give honor to his patron.

> Herm [. . . (to Sarapion)], greetings, and that you may always remain in good health in your whole person for long years to come, since your good genius allowed us to greet you with respect and salute you. For as you also make mention of us on each occasion by letter, so I here make an act of worship for you in the presence of the lords Dioskouroi and the presence of the lord Sarapis, and I pray for your safekeeping during your entire life and for the health of your children and all your household. Farewell in everything, I beg, my patron and fosterer. Greet all your folk, men and women. All the gods here, male and female, greet you. Farewell. Thoth 16th. *(Verso)* To Sarapion, the lord. (Transl. by G. H. R. Horsley, *NDIEC* (1981), p. 57)

In modern society the private spheres of friendship and family are segregated from the public spheres of labor and politics. In classical thought, friendship was the basis of politics, and the family was the basis of economic activity. The classical Greek and Roman concepts of friendship were different, but by the first century C.E. the former had greatly influenced the latter. In classical Greece, boys were socialized outside the home in a male group of the same age. This same-age same-sex group later became the basis for a hetaery (Greek, *hetairia*), a union of friends. The hetaery was a political faction and the most important force in Greek politics. In classical thought the basis of friendship and political groups (also military groups) was eros, male sexuality. There is much evidence that the male bond was often stronger than heterosexual relationships, especially among aristocrats. In many spheres of life, men and women were strictly separated.

Friends were to be equals; equality was to characterize the relationship. An ancient maxim said that friends shared all things in common. The ideals of Greek male friendship greatly influenced ancient epistolography. Throughout antiquity, theorists asserted that the genre of the letter was epitomized by the friendly letter. In spite of the fact that the letter was extensively used far beyond the domain of Greek friendship, writers continued to speak as if the only true letter was the friendly letter. A group of motifs and clichés derived from classical Greek friendship became part of the standard content of the letter. It is doubtful that any but those with some wealth and leisure could attain either the Greek or the Roman ideal of friendship. The sharing of two selves, which was a classical definition of friendship, was also used to characterize the function of the letter; the letter permitted absent friends to share in one another. Seneca writes to Lucilius:

> I thank you for writing to me so often; for you are revealing your real self to me in the only way you can. I never receive a letter from you without being in your company forthwith. If the pictures of our absent friends are pleasing to us, though they only refresh the memory and lighten our longing by a solace that is unreal and unsubstantial, how much more pleasant is a letter, which brings us real traces, real evidences, of an absent friend! For that which is sweetest when we meet face to face is afforded by the impress of a friend's hand upon his letter—recognition. (*Moral Letters* 40.1)[3]

Latin letter writers adopted the conventions and friendly ethos of Greek letter writing. One finds the same motifs and clichés from Greek friendship in Latin letters, in spite of the fact that the Roman concept of friendship, *amicitia,* was different. Traditionally, the concept of *amicitia* did not emphasize sentiment and male affection as the Greek concept did. *Amicitia* was also firmly anchored in the Roman family and the alliance of families. It was often an alliance of utility between social equals and was sometimes equated with "political party" *(factio)*. Traditionally, then, it was the chief horizontal relationship between influential people in contrast to the vertical, hierarchical client-patron relationship. In practice, however, socially aspiring clients were sometimes called friends *(amici)* since, as Cicero writes *(On Duties* 2.69), those with aristocratic pretensions considered the appellation "client" worse than death. The conventions of *amicitia* were backed by very powerful social sanctions. A breach of these norms involved a loss of dignity *(dignitas)* and honor *(gloria)*.

In Hellenistic and Roman times there was no longer a central political role for Greek friendship. There was thus a tendency to broaden the concept and often detach it from specifically male companionship. Plutarch even advocated the classically unthinkable idea that wives could be friends. Some Jewish writers such as Philo and Josephus found a broadened view of Greek friendship acceptable. Jewish traditions, like the Roman, tended to emphasize the family and heterosexual relationships in a way that made the classical Greek ideal of friendship uncongenial.

In sum, then, Greek friendship was widely influential in a broadened way and deeply impressed the Hellenistic and Roman letter-writing traditions. A fuller expression of the Greek ideal is found in the letters of the educated and leisured upper strata of society than in the lower. Friendship was considered to be the basis for politics. As Cicero's letters to Atticus and others illustrate, political discussion is quite natural to the friendly letter. Theorists tended to suggest that the true and genuine function of the letter genre was as a vehicle for expressing and maintaining the sharing and affections of friendship. In reality, however, the letter had attained much broader uses.

In spite of the theorists, Greek and Roman letters are often dominated more by the language and ethos of family than of friendship. This is especially the case for the papyrus letters from Egypt and the earliest Christian letters. The term "family," however, can be misleading because the ancient household differed greatly from the modern family. The modern family consists of husband, wife, and unmarried children. For the most part, the modern family is a sphere of privacy separated from politics, economic activity, and education, which take place outside the home. The modern family is a mobile and independent social group. Its members are individuals, and the specialization of functions among members and the role of biological bonds have been greatly deemphasized in the twentieth century. In all these respects, ancient families or households were quite different.

Greek, Roman, and Jewish households were normally large and complex social hierarchies. At the top was the highest-ranking male, the Greek lord *(kyrios)* or Roman paterfamilias. He was often likened to a king ruling over his kingdom. All power and legal control was through him. Next were his wife and children. The patriarch's married sons with wives and children were also part of the household. Depending on ethnic custom, social class, and historical period, the married sons may or may not have actually lived in the same house. Under the immediate blood relatives came slaves, hired servants, live-in guests, and associated freedmen and freedwomen. According to ancient thought, a genuine and often a legal household did not exist without slaves. Households were related to other households through complex alliances often based on traditional kinship associations, ties of *amicitia,* or client-patron relationships.

For Jews, Romans, and the lower strata of Greeks, most education and socialization took place within the household. Business and economic activity was also centered within the household. This is why ancients could not conceive of a household without slaves. Just as one expects to find politics in friendly letters, one also expects to find business matters in familial letters. This fact is amply illustrated in the papyrus letters.

It is the activities associated with friendship, client-patron relationships, and the household that generated most of the letters which we have from antiquity. Christian letters also fit into these contexts, but with modifications created by the institutions and ethos of the church. All three forms of social relationships played important roles within the developing life of the Christian groups of antiquity. Most Christian letter writing is understandable within these contexts.

3

Education, Art,
and Professional Letter Writing

The standard account of Greek and Roman education gives it three stages: elementary school, secondary school with the *grammaticus* as teacher, and rhetorical training. For several reasons this account is seriously misleading. First there was great local variation depending upon available resources and needs, especially outside the major cities. Many places had only an elementary teacher, who taught basic reading and writing and occasionally, if he was able, also some classical literature. Second, the supposed stages of education were not generally successive but often socially differentiated tracks, especially in major cities. The elementary schools taught by the "teacher of letters" were generally attended only by the lower classes. Boys from the upper classes either learned to read and write at home or began their elementary education with the grammaticus. Only those who had studied with a grammaticus could go on to a teacher of rhetoric.

Thus there was not usually a movement from the "teacher of letters" to the grammaticus. As shown by hundreds of papyri and ostraca (potsherds written on with pen and ink), the instruction of the grammaticus centered on the analysis and imitation of the classics of history, literature, and oratory. Often, however, he provided his typically upper-class students with their elementary instruction in reading and writing.

Letter writing was learned in the secondary stage of education, although we do not know how widespread this instruction was or exactly what was taught. Grammatical handbooks show a passing interest in letter writing and presuppose a knowledge of basic forms. The elementary exercises in rhetoric *(progymnasmata)* were also taught to various degrees in secondary education, although rhetoricians were not inclined to relinquish to the grammarian any but the most elementary exercises. The progymnastic exercises of

Theon and Nicolaus say that letter writing is a useful exercise for developing characterization and impersonation of style. Nicolaus notes that this is so because letters ought to portray the personalities of the writers and recipients. Some fictitious letters from antiquity may have been written as progymnastic exercises in characterization. This exercise undoubtedly contributed to the popularity of pseudonymous letters.

Like most other instruction in antiquity, letter writing was taught by the imitation of models rather than through theory and comprehensive rules. Model papyrus letters from Egypt date as far back as the second century B.C.E. *Papyrus Bononiensis* 5 is the exercises of a student in writing various types of letters. The student probably followed a handbook. It is written on a rather elementary level by someone with modest linguistic skills. Each letter has been copied in both Greek and Latin. The following is a congratulatory letter from the exercises of this unknown student of letter writing:

> Happily, brother, do I congratulate you for having paid close attention to my recommendation in the exposure of Quintus. I heard that this matter was expedited and how it was quite worthy of you. But, oh, your modesty and self-control! I delight in your very character, since in this you repaid us. But I have an (outstanding) debt. What, then, is it? I hope soon to give you an accounting of this obligation of yours.[4]

Professional letter writers served government bureaucracies, well-to-do households, and the largely illiterate wider public. In a letter to Nicobulus that gives advice on writing letters, Gregory of Nazianzus mentions that Nicobulus can learn more from "those skilled in such matters." Gregory is probably referring to a sort of business-school teacher who trained people in such things as stenography and letter writing as preparation especially for the civil service. Contracts for the training of professional writers have been discovered among the papyri. A handbook under the name of Demetrius is addressed to a writer of official letters, although most of the twenty-one types of letters it discusses are not official ones. This and similar handbooks may have been used in the training and work of professional letter writers. The handbook of Demetrius and another under the name of Libanius (sometimes Proclus) also show considerable interest in rhetorical topics and in defining types of exhortation.

The highest level of linguistic and literary achievement came to those who completed the secondary stage of education and then studied with a teacher of rhetoric. Greco-Roman culture regarded the well-delivered and persuasive speech as the most characteristic feature of civilized life. In contrast to our own culture, linguistic skill focused on oral speech; the written word was secondary, derived from primary rhetoric.

Letter writing remained only on the fringes of formal rhetorical education throughout antiquity. It was never integrated into the rhetorical systems and thus does not appear in the standard handbooks. This means there were never any detailed systematic rules for letters, as there were for standard rhetorical forms. The rules for certain types of speeches, however, were adapted for use in corresponding letter types. So, for example, a letter of consolation written by a person with rhetorical training may more or less follow the form of the consolatory speech.

The earliest extant rhetorical work that treats letter writing is the book *On Style,* attributed to Demetrius of Phalerum and probably dating from the first century B.C.E. Its discussion reflects well-developed traditions and conventions about the letter as an expression of Greek friendship. At about the same time, Cicero reflects the thorough assimilation of these traditions into the educated Roman world. The great Latin letter writers—such as Cicero, Ovid, Seneca, Pliny, Fronto—were all thoroughly trained in the rhetorical schools. In the early third century C.E., Philostratus of Lemnos wrote a work on how to write letters. His now-lost book reflected controversies among rhetoricians concerning proper epistolary usage by letter writers in government service. Julius Victor appended a discussion of letter writing to his rhetorical handbook in the fourth century. The handbooks of Demetrius and Libanius on letter writing betray close acquaintance with the issues and definitions of the rhetoricians.

Of the numerous uses to which letters were put, one use very naturally has dominated the modern study of Greco-Roman letters. That is the employment of the letter as a means of aesthetic expression. Modern classicism and the study of classical literature in the schools has focused on literary artistry in letters. This makes it difficult to grasp the fact that such aestheticism belonged to an extremely small group of writers, who lived in a rarefied world of elite sensitivities. It was the study of rhetoric which developed these sensitivities, and it was the cultivation of these classical aesthetic interests which most distinguishes the letter writing of certain later Christian authors like Gregory of Nazianzus or Jerome from Paul or Ignatius. Beginning in the second century, the great models of artistic letter writing were produced by Greek sophists such as Dio

Chrysostom, Philostratus, and Libanius. In style, Christian writers like Gregory and Jerome resemble these pagan sophists.

The social context for such literary letters is a small circle of intimate aristocratic friends who share advanced rhetorical educations. The purpose is aesthetic entertainment. As Pliny remarks, the first requirement for this kind of literary activity is leisure (*Letter* 7.2). Pliny notes that such letters should usually be brief and employ simple vocabulary in a direct style (*Letter* 7.9.8). The paradox is that Pliny employs elaborate structure and studied prose rhythm in order to achieve this simplicity and directness. Pliny refers to the gatherings of friends where such literary gems were shared. Horace's and Ovid's poetic letters are another aesthetic development of the letter.

In the fourth and fifth centuries, Christian writers with the requisite aristocratic and educational backgrounds for such activity begin to appear. The subject matter is somewhat different, and traditional aristocratic leisure is replaced by the monastic leisure of the contemplative life, but the same kind of aestheticism appears in some Christian letters. Gregory of Nazianzus tells Nicobulus that one of the most important qualities of a letter is its charm, which is to be achieved by the moderate use of rhetorical embellishment (*Letter* 51). Gregory of Nyssa gushes with praise for a letter he has received from the pagan sophist Libanius (*Letter* 14). The charm and beauty of the letter was so impressive to him that he joyously shared it with his friends. Synesius, bishop of Cyrene, writes to Pylaemenes concerning the latter's epistle: "I read it with both pleasure and admiration; for it is worthy because of its expression of your soul and its beauty of language. I quickly gathered an audience of Libyan Greeks for you and told them to come and hear an eloquent letter."[5]

Such literati set the standards for literary excellence, including letter writing. The historian, however, is obliged not to allow their canons of taste to obscure the larger phenomenon of letter writing. It has especially been tempting for some to equate the "real" letter with the aesthetically oriented friendly letter, as literary writers did in antiquity. That is one very significant type of letter from one social context.

4

Philosophy
and Character Formation

The articulation of theories and methods of moral education and character formation was primarily the work of philosophy in antiquity. Rhetoric, however, continued to influence and be influenced by philosophy. Rhetoricians, for example, sometimes provided moral education when they emphasized the ethos of the speaker. Rhetoric also transmitted traditional Greek folk morality and popular teaching methods. The various philosophies both used and criticized these traditions in their more systematic moral theories. These moral and pedagogical traditions were very important for early Christianity. The kinds of letters that figure most prominently in early Christianity were types used especially by those who pursued the philosophical life.

Since Kant, philosophy has been professionalized into a largely academic discipline focusing on theories of knowledge. Philosophy in antiquity was quite different. Philosophy was the pursuit of wisdom in living. The practical goals of ancient philosophy were the virtuous and happy life, whether through the individual efforts of the Stoic sage or the ideal state of the early Academy. The model philosopher in antiquity was Socrates, a man who never wrote a book but who taught a way of living by his own life and death. After Socrates, the task of philosophy was to care for the soul. The philosopher was to tend his own soul and those of others in order to make them as good as possible.

Each philosophy had its own teachings about the nature of the world, the human predicament, and the philosophical cure for that predicament. Their literatures and teaching methods varied according to their differing beliefs. Some Cynic philosophers believed that people were so deeply trapped in vice that only the harshest censure and rebuke could effect a cure. Other Cynics and other philosophical schools argued that such a regimen would kill the patient; rather, the philosopher ought to be gentle and adapt his speech to each individual's condition.

The philosopher's first task was to persuade people to adopt the philosophical life. In theory, at least, all philosophical sects stood in tension with normal society. This varied according to the beliefs of the particular school, and consequently so did the radicalness of the call to the philosophical life. Cynics rejected normal society as unnatural and perverted; Stoics tended to spiritualize a Cynic-like detachment while at the same time supporting the social and political order; Epicureans withdrew and formed their own communities of friends.

The acceptance of a philosophy was often experienced as a conversion to a new and better way of life. In the following fragment from some now-lost comic play, a man who has perhaps come to Athens in order to hear the philosophers describes his conversion.

> Believe me, O men, my whole life until now has been death rather than life. All was shadow: The beautiful, the holy, the good was evil; such was the earlier darkness of my understanding that it seems all of these things were hidden and veiled. But now, since I have come here, I have come back to life just as if I had slept in a temple of Asclepius and he had cured me for the rest of my life. I walk, I talk, I understand. The sun, so great and magnificent, O men, I have discovered anew; I now see you, the sky, the acropolis and the theater in the clear light of today.[6]

Going back at least to Aristotle's famous *Protrepticus* there was a long tradition of putting exhortations to the philosophical life into the form of letters. Conversion literature in the Greco-Roman world came from philosophy and not the Greek and Roman religious cults, which offered myths and rituals but not an articulated worldview and a way of life.

Usually the initial conversion, whether a quiet commitment or a dramatic transformation, was not considered to be enough. The aspiring student needed a philosophical guide or a doctor of the soul. In the third Cynic letter of Pseudo-Diogenes, Diogenes offers himself to Hipparchia as a philosophical guide. This relationship is to be carried on by means of letters:

> I admire you for your eagerness in that, although you are a woman, you yearned for philosophy and have become one of our school, which has struck even men with awe for its austerity. But be earnest to bring to a finish what you have begun. And you will cap it off, I am sure, if you should not be outstripped

by Crates, your husband, and if you frequently write to me, your benefactor in philosophy. For letters are worth a great deal and are not inferior to conversation with people actually present.[7]

The writer of this letter was not alone in considering the letter to be a preeminent means of philosophical pedagogy. The letter was one of the most characteristic means of expression for ancient philosophy. But why? The philosopher's purpose was not to inform. Even when information about philosophical dogmas is given, a moral purpose is usually in view. We possess a few truly didactic letters, such as Epicurus' letters to Pythocles and Herodotus, but numerous hortatory letters from philosophers. The primary purpose of the philosophical hortatory letter is to affect the habits and dispositions of the reader(s) according to a certain model of what it means to be human. A hortatory letter from an official (quite rare) to a subordinate would be similar in some ways but more restricted in scope since it would have primarily a model of the good subordinate official in view.

What was important was not abstract information but living models of character who embodied philosophical doctrines. Seneca writes to Lucilius as his philosophical guide in *Moral Letters* 6.3–5:

> You cannot conceive what distinct progress I notice that each day brings to me. And when you say: "Give me also a share in these gifts which you have found so helpful," I reply that I am anxious to heap all these privileges upon you, and that I am glad to learn in order that I may teach. . . . Of course, however, the living voice and the intimacy of a common life will help you more than the written word. You must go to the scene of action, first, because men put more faith in their eyes than in their ears, and second, because the way is long if one follows precepts, but short and helpful, if one follows examples.[8]

The letter was the literary genre through which the living example of the guide and the shared lives of teacher and student could best be communicated.

Demetrius, *On Style*, writes:

> The letter, like the dialogue, should abound in glimpses of character. It may be said that everybody reveals his own soul in his letters. In every other form of composition it is possible to discern the writer's character, but in none so clearly as in the epistolary.[9]

As the student of rhetoric was to imitate the oratory of his teacher, so the student of philosophy was to imitate the character of his mentor. The letter, above all, was the genre that expressed character.

The student of philosophy was to learn by sharing the conversation and friendship of his guide. As in the letter of Crates quoted above, the letter was supposed to be dialogical or conversational in style. The student-teacher relationship in philosophy was not like that of the grammaticus and his boys. It was the relationship of an older and wiser friend to a younger and less mature friend. Friendship was the social form of ancient philosophical groups. The letter, of course, was above all viewed as a means for maintaining friendship. The conversation of exchanged letters made the student and his guide present to one another. Through the letter, the guide exhorted, corrected, and advised. It was a commonplace that a true friend was distinguishable from a flatterer because the friend would admonish and rebuke when necessary while the flatterer would only praise and encourage. Thus, philosophical correspondences typically contain various letters of encouragement, admonition, and rebuke. Positive and negative exhortation were considered to be complementary. The skillful philosophical guide knew when to use and how to combine the many varieties of exhortation.

The extensive letter-writing activity of philosophical groups in antiquity began with the disciples of Socrates. Only letters of Plato survive from that group, although others were well known and admired in antiquity. Plato's Academy was a group of friends. In accordance with Greek friendship they were a male political party. Plato believed that the Socratic guidance of souls could only come about through a polis, a Greek city-state, designed and governed by philosophers. Plato traveled to several places attempting to establish his ideal polis. He also sent letters encouraging, rebuking, and advising his disciples in various places. In Letter 6, for example, he exhorts followers in Atarneus to practice the true friendship and fellowship of philosophy.

Epicurus reacted against the political philosophy of Plato. He became convinced that the party strife, violence, and state religion of the polis was unnatural and dehumanizing. Epicurus' radical alternative was withdrawal from the life of the polis into communities of "natural friendship" which repudiated the Greek pursuit of honor and renown. Epicurus even allowed women into his semi-ascetic communities. Early in his career he moved from Asia Minor to Athens. From there he maintained communication with scattered communities of disciples in Asia Minor and elsewhere by means of letters. He addresses one letter "to the philosophers in Mytilene"; another "to friends in Lampsacus." The first city is on the island of Lesbos off the coast of Asia Minor; the second farther north on the Hellespont, which divides Asia Minor from Europe. He exhorted, encouraged, gave advice, settled disputes, taught his doctrines, and maintained fellowship through his letters. Letters served Epicurus much as they did Paul almost four hundred years later.

The Stoics, who were the dominant school in the Hellenistic age and early empire, produced many letters, most of which are lost. Cynics were active in the early Hellenistic age and throughout the empire until they became indistinguishable from Christian monks. An extensive collection of fictitious Cynic letters written in the names of earlier sages has survived. The letter lent itself to such fictitious correspondences in philosophical circles. In form such letters are often difficult to distinguish from genuine correspondences. Using fictitious letters, the writer could take advantage of the characteristics of the letter for more general exhortation and pedagogy. Thus, the personality of Diogenes in the fictitious letters of Diogenes becomes a model for a certain view of what it means to be a Cynic. These letters are directed widely toward Cynic circles.

Seneca, the eclectic Stoic, wrote a series of 124 letters to Lucilius. By current consensus this correspondence, at least in its present form, is also a literary fiction. Whether genuine or imaginary, however, the letters realistically depict Seneca's guidance of Lucilius' spiritual development by means of epistolary paraenesis. They are a valuable aid to our understanding of philosophical paraenesis because they depict development over a period of time.

From the second century C.E. onward there was a period of sweeping cultural change which scholars have designated "late antiquity." In this period, a new and often otherworldly Platonism became the dominant philosophy. The new Platonism owed much to Stoicism and Cynicism in its ethics. This mix was congenial to educated Christians. We find letters characteristic of philosophy produced in later antiquity not only by pagan Platonists but also by Christians such as Gregory of Nyssa, Augustine, and Synesius. In this period, philosophy and rhetoric reached a synthesis that was the characteristic mark of both educated pagan and Christian writers.

5

Letters in Jewish
and Early Christian Communities

The Semitic-speaking cultures of the East had letter-writing traditions of their own. Some of these letters are found in the Hebrew Bible (e.g., 2 Sam. 11:14–15; 1 Kings 21:8–10; 2 Kings 10:1–6; 19:9, 14; Ezra 4–5). A large proportion of these are official letters like the one from the Jewish settlement in Elephantine, Egypt, to the Persian governor of Judea requesting help against attacks on the Jewish temple at Elephantine by Egyptian priests. Elephantine was a military colony of Jewish mercenaries that guarded the southern Egyptian frontier for the Persians. These Jews had their own temple and did not observe the Mosaic law known in the Pentateuch. None of these letters, however, resemble the Pauline epistles or, in general, other early Christian letters aside from common papyrus letters written by Christians about everyday matters.

By the first century c.e., more Jews lived in cities of the Roman empire outside Galilee and Judea than within. Most of these Jews spoke Greek and were just as Greek in culture as Jews living in the United States are American in culture; they were also at least as diverse in their forms of Judaism. (This analogy is fair if not pushed too far. The modern nation-state is obviously different from ancient Hellenism.) All of the writers of the New Testament letters were probably Jews. As far as we know, none of the Christian letter writers outside the New Testament were Jews. The Christian letter-writing tradition received a strong and lasting initial influence from Hellenistic Jewish letter writers.

Aside from purely religious thought, Jewish traditions made a permanent impress on Christian letters in the use of Old Testament language, prayers, thanksgivings, and blessings. Paul, the Hellenistic Jew, provided the most important models for Christian letters until Gregory of Nazianzus and Basil became the most imitated letter writers in the Byzantine church. From such sources as Philo,

Josephus, and 1 and 2 Maccabees we know of extensive Jewish letter-writing activity in the Hellenistic period and the early empire. Letters, however, never became the preeminent—or even a significant—form of normative religious expression for Judaism that they did for Christianity. There is only one certain letter in the whole Talmud (B. *Sanhedrin* 11a).

Through their Judaism, the earliest Christians bequeathed the self-identity of resident aliens to later Christians. Jews of the Diaspora were alien nationals living permanently in the cities and towns of the Roman empire. Christians thought of themselves as the third race, neither Greek nor Jewish. This meant that they were to form their own self-governing communities. They would mark their own celebrations and write their own literature. In the first three centuries C.E., this drive toward social self-definition produced remarkably diverse forms of Christianity. Perhaps it is best to speak of Christianities in this period. The next three centuries are just as remarkable for their movement toward political and theological consolidation and uniformity. With any generalization about early Christian letter writing, an exception lurks just around the corner.

Many Christian groups had, on the one hand, the character-building goals that made Epicureanism a letter-writing movement and, on the other hand, the supralocal organizational impulse that made letter writing essential for the Roman imperial administration. The first of these is well illustrated by the letters of Paul and his followers. Here, complex paraenetic or hortatory letters of various types predominate. In many ways, these resemble hortatory philosophical letters. Paul knows and uses the terms for and techniques of different kinds of exhortation. In describing his missionary work with the Thessalonians, he says, "You know how, like a father with his children, we exhorted each one of you and encouraged you and charged you" (1 Thess. 2:11). Paul continued his hortatory activity with the Thessalonians after he left by means of letters.

In two respects, Paul's character-building through hortatory letters differed widely from that of the Epicureans and other philosophical groups. Paul's focus is not on individual character but on building communities. Individuals are exhorted to have virtues and dispositions that contribute to the life of the community. Members are mutually to build one another up. Second, Paul attributes this achievement of community life and Christian character to God's power and activity. The classical ideal of friendship is not and could not have been expressed in Paul's letters. Circles of friends were associations of individual social equals bound by similarity of social background and political or philosophical goals. Even in Epicurean groups, the community existed for the private spiritual goals of each individual. In the Pauline letters, there is a strongly communal goal.

Although some conventions from the friendly letter do appear in the Pauline letters, a family ethos strongly predominates. Some of this is traceable to Judaism but the ethos is also strongly reminiscent of the common papyrus familial letter. The church is often described as a household. Paul builds and maintains this family through his letters. He aids in governing mostly by giving advice and settling disputes. He articulates norms of self-definition and behavior. He teaches and shares in worship through his letters.

Exhortation and advice also dominate the other New Testament letters. As among philosophical groups, letters written in the name of renowned teachers are used for paraenesis. In the pastoral epistles, for example, Paul becomes a model of the bold but gentle teacher and community builder, as he exhorts Timothy and Titus to the same behavior. False teachers who use evil methods are censured to provide a contrasting negative hortatory model. Third John very much resembles a common papyrus letter as the writer commends certain travelers and censures a certain Diotrephes. James loosely strings together very generalized precepts and exhortations without any specific paraenetic advice.

The writings of the so-called apostolic fathers, i.e., the letters of Ignatius and Polycarp and the first letter of Clement, are also primarily letters of exhortation and advice. On his way to martyrdom in Rome, Ignatius urges churches along the way to close ranks behind a strong organization of single bishops, each of whom is to rule over the church in his area with an advising board of elders under him. In time, the church would have an organization of bishops and archbishops that mirrored the organization of the Roman empire. After Constantine's conversion, many emperors strengthened and promoted the power of bishops. It is no surprise, then, that letters from bishops concerning the governance of the church became characteristic in the fourth and fifth centuries.

As hortatory letters dominate the remains from first- and second-century letter writing, so judicial and deliberative rhetoric comes to the fore in bishops' letters of the fourth and fifth centuries. Later bishops often held a sort of small claims court as well as ecclesiastical courts and performed many judicial functions. There are, for example, letters of excommunication and removal of excommunication (e.g., Synesius, *Letters* 12, 58). Bishops are often petitioned and answer petitions with letters. Letters which censure heretics and polemicize against their ideas are very prominent as are apologetic letters that attempt to defend beliefs and practices. In the fourth and fifth centuries, hortatory letters become a prominent tool for advocates of the monastic life.

Dionysius, bishop of Corinth in the late second century, provides a useful illustration of the types of letters bishops wrote in the earlier period. In a slightly anachronistic account, Eusebius describes his prolific correspondence (*History of the Church* 4.23). He is said to have sent a hortatory letter of advice and instruction to the Lacedaemonians on the subject of peace and unity. To the Athenians, he sent a letter calling for renewal of faith and sharply reproving them for their failures. Another of Dionysius' letters was addressed to the church in the Bithynian capital, Nicomedia, in order to combat the charismatic sect of Montanism. One, to churches on Crete, praises a certain bishop and exhorts them to guard against heretical teachings. A letter requested by two men in Pontus contained scriptural exegesis and paraenesis concerning marriage. Another letter exhorted the bishop of Cnossus not to burden brethren with ascetic practices. The bishop of Cnossus wrote in return, exhorting Dionysius to send another letter which would encourage his members to what he considered a more advanced form of piety. He wrote to the Roman church praising Soter, the bishop, for the churches' benevolent activities and hospitality. He also told the Romans that the Corinthian church still publicly read the letter of advice and admonition which had been written by Clement on behalf of the Roman church seventy years earlier and sent to Corinth. Dionysius says that the Corinthians still received admonition from hearing the letter.

It is clear from the example of Dionysius and other early writers that the letter was an extremely important tool for the changing church. It was no longer a matter of the lone itinerant apostle and his fellow workers struggling to build several small churches over a large area. Now there was a network of churches often led by articulate bishops which mutually supported and sometimes feuded with one another. Belief, religious practice, and the social fabric of these communities were developed and maintained over distances through letters. The writers whose works were important enough to have been preserved or mentioned by the later church are either official leaders of the churches or educated Christians who were often described as teachers. The latter were independent of official church organization and often resembled philosophical teachers. Such people as Justin Martyr, Tatian, Valentinus, Pantaenus, and Origen collected groups of students around them on the model of philosophical schools. We know that many of these were prolific letter writers. Through letters, the bishops, elders, deacons, and teachers sought consensus through dialogue and conflict. They drew boundaries of developing self-definition; they gave praise and blame to one another; they developed an articulated religious philosophy for the church; they defended the churches against outside attack; they advised one another and gave various sorts of exhortation to strengthen the communities from within.

In the Latin West, Cyprian, bishop of Carthage, was a prolific letter writer in the middle of the third century. Cyprian had been a pagan rhetorician converted later in life. He employs both the hortatory tradition and the judicial rhetoric of the Roman legal tradition. Cyprian fled into exile during the persecution by the emperor Decian in 249 but continued to pastor his church by means of letters. Some in Rome accused Cyprian of abandoning his church. In a letter of defense addressed to the elders and deacons at Rome, Cyprian defends himself by describing how he was able to continue his responsibilities with letters. For proof, he appends thirteen letters written to his church during that time. Cyprian says that he used letters to give advice, exhort and encourage, rebuke, give consolation, and persuade. It is clear that Cyprian viewed his pastoral letter writing largely in terms of giving various sorts of exhortation. His judicial rhetoric shows itself in his controversial apologetic and polemical letters such as the violent correspondence between him and Stephen, bishop of Rome, concerning whether heretics could administer baptism.

We possess thousands of letters from the golden age of Christian letter writing in the second half of the fourth and the fifth centuries. To Isidore of Pelusium alone are attributed more than two thousand letters. The writers of this age also include Athanasius, Ambrose, Ausonius, Gregory of Nazianzus, Basil, Gregory of Nyssa, John Chrysostom, Synesius, Jerome, Augustine, Paulinus of Nola, Sidonius, and Theodoret. The field is so vast that only a few observations are possible here.

These writers achieved a synthesis of classical rhetoric and Christian traditions best exemplified in the East by Gregory of Nazianzus and in the West by Jerome and Augustine. Isidore of Pelusium expresses this ideal of critical acceptance of classical culture in Letter 3.65. He says that classical grammar, rhetoric, and philosophy have fallen away from the truth. But, "if these arts are made beautiful by the truth" (i.e., Christianity), they are properly desired by the wise.

The high social and educational levels of these writers, together with changes in the church, distinguish their letters from earlier extant Christian letters. The church became more and more hierarchical and more clearly mirrored the social structure of the empire. The typical social contexts of letter writing now appear more clearly reflected in Christian writers. The authors of the golden age had advanced rhetorical and philosophical educations and often came from aristocratic backgrounds. Paul's style would not have been considered acceptable by these Christian authors if he had written in their day. The church itself had a distinct social pyramid and had developed its own peculiar life-contexts which regularly generated specific types of letters, e.g., doctrinal controversy, worship, church government, monastic life.

All of the classical traditions of the friendly letter now appear in correspondences. Friendly letters became typical of educated monks and bishops. A few, such as Basil and Paulinus of Nola, developed a critical view of the tradition and contrasted Christian brotherly love to friendship. Typically, however, the friendly letter not only appears but is also used to maintain relationships of *amicitia* or an ascetic Greek friendship. Being rhetorically trained, these authors show a marked ability to widely vary their styles and letter types to fit the occasion. Hortatory and philosophical letters are still important, as are sermon-like letters which combine exhortation and deliberative rhetoric. Epideictic forms such as *encomia* and *consolations* are frequently adapted to letters. Finally, vituperative, apologetical, and polemical letters of various sorts employing judicial and deliberative rhetoric are widely used in theological controversies.

Bishops and holy men play the role of patron in the fourth and fifth centuries. It is likely that patrons were always of importance to the church. In the letters of Paul, churches seem to be organized around the households of well-to-do patrons like Gaius (Rom. 16: 23). As the household and patronage were probably the important social forms in the first century, so patronage and friendship were central social forms in the fourth and fifth centuries out of which much letter writing was generated. Letters of recommendation and intercession, for example, are extremely numerous in the correspondences of the writers mentioned above. Typically, these letters consist of a recommendation or intercession from one friend to another on behalf of a client. Patrons were spiritual superiors who acted as mediators for both worldly and spiritual favors. Clients usually wrote supplicatory letters filled with praise.

It was by means of letters that local disputes became empire-wide theological controversies. When Arius, an elder, became involved in a controversy with Alexander, his bishop in Alexandria, he responded by disseminating his ideas all over the East by letter. He thus picked up a powerful supporter in Eusebius of Nicomedia. Alexander in turn called a local synod, excommunicated Arius and wrote letters to bishops throughout the church condemning him. That was the beginning of the Arian controversy which would rip and contort the church for centuries. When the emperor Constantine wrote, ordering Arius and the bishop Alexander to stop feuding and to be reconciled, it was already too late. Leaders throughout the church had already begun to take sides.

Following the precedent of the apostolic council in Acts 15, synods and councils regularly sent official letters often called "tomes." Sometimes these were letters of decree which resemble imperial letters and sometimes they were didactic letters which set forth theological positions. It is well to remember that the extant epistolary remains from the tradition of theological controversy are not a matter of fortuitous preservation. The letters of those who won theological controversies, and were thus declared orthodox, were preserved. For the most part, the writings of the losers ended up in the fire.

I have already mentioned friendly letters for the purpose of aesthetic entertainment. Ausonius composed poetic Latin epistles but little that is specifically Christian comes through. Specifically Christian forms were developed such as the festal letters which became popular in the late fourth and fifth centuries. This practice began in Alexandria where the bishop would announce the beginning of the Easter season in a hortatory pastoral letter to his church.

In contrast to these letters of rhetorically educated church leaders are the papyrus letters by more ordinary Christians. These have been preserved in considerable number beginning in the third century. These are mostly common familial and business letters by people either illiterate or barely literate. Very often the senders are only identifiable as Christian by a reference to the Lord, Christ, or God, instead of the gods, in one of the opening or closing formulas such as the prayer, thanksgiving, or wish for health. Since monasticism began in Egypt, there are also a considerable number of letters to and from abbots concerning the day-to-day life of monastic communities. These date mostly from the fifth century. Holy men are sometimes petitioned for prayer and healing or approached as patrons in papyrus letters. The papyrus letters help us to catch a sound from the voice of the common Christian which has been all but lost in the glory of the great letter writers of the golden age.

PART TWO
Types of Letters

If we are to understand Greco-Roman letter writing, we must closely study specific types of letters rather than merely consider "the letter" abstractly. In studying types of letters we must necessarily take note of their functions in Greco-Roman society. A far greater number of types were used by early Christians and in the larger society than we can discuss here. We can, however, study some of the most important kinds of letters and understand the principles by which the ancients classified letters and specified types. This requires a grasp of the complex interrelationship between rhetorical theory, literary tradition, moral philosophy, and the practice of letter writing.

6

Understanding Epistolary Types

Greco-Roman rhetoricians divided the genus of rhetoric into three species: judicial (or forensic), deliberative (or advising) and epideictic (or panegyric). There are types of letters which belong to each of the three species. Other types of letters do not easily fit any of the three species. The first step in grasping the relationship between types of letters and rhetoric is to understand the limitations of rhetorical classification.

Following Aristotle, the three species were defined as the speech of three different social contexts. *Judicial* rhetoric was, of course, the rhetoric of the courtroom. It concerned decisions about what was just or unjust in the past. *Deliberative* or advisory speaking was the rhetoric of the governing assembly or council. Deliberative speaking concerned what course of action would be expedient or useful in the future, e.g., should we go to war or stay at peace. *Epideictic* was the rhetoric of praise and blame for customary occasions such as victory celebrations, weddings, and funerals. Its purpose was to make clear what was honorable and what was shameful.

In the schools and in practice, most of the rhetoric in antiquity was judicial. Theory and practice was most fully developed for the courtroom. On the one hand, epideictic was the species that was most neglected in theory and in handbooks. On the other hand, it became a catch-all category for every type of rhetoric which did not fit into judicial or deliberative. Rhetorical theory was always a combination of what actually happened in practice and what the rhetoricians thought ought to be the case. Some rhetoricians openly admitted that the categories were somewhat artificial and tended to overlap ("Cicero," *To Herennius* 3.4.7; Quintilian, *Education of the Orator* 3.4.15–16). Cicero and Quintilian also rightly noted that works on rhetoric almost entirely omitted the treatment of exhorta-

51

tion (Cicero, *On the Orator* 2.64; Quintilian, *Education of the Orator* 3.4.2–9).

Two types of letters, the accusing and the apologetic, clearly fall under judicial rhetoric. The letter of advice would also clearly seem to belong to deliberative rhetoric. Most other kinds of letters could be conceived of as belonging to epideictic, which had two departments, praise and blame. If one, for example, considers the "types" of Demetrius and the "styles" of Libanius, their categories fit epideictic fairly well. Under letters of praise fall commendation, consolation, praising, congratulations, thanking, erotic, and diplomatic. Under letters of blame are the following types: blaming, reproaching, censure, admonition, threatening, vituperation, reproach, reproof, and the ironic letter which is feigned praise that is actually blame. The paraenetic letter and the friendly letter can combine both praise and blame.

The classification of letter types according to the three species of rhetoric only partially works. This is because the letter-writing tradition was essentially independent of rhetoric. Furthermore, many of the letter types correspond to kinds of exhortation (paraenesis), and exhortation was only tangentially related to rhetorical theory. In fact, the most systematic treatment of exhortation was in moral philosophy.

This pedagogical rhetoric of philosophy culminated in Posidonius, who systemized exhortation into a "department of practical ethics" (i.e., *paraenesis*, translated by Seneca as *praeceptio* or *pars praeceptiva*). Posidonius conceived of three major types of paraenesis, corresponding to the three aspects of the moral life: advice was for actions, exhortation for character or habit, and consolation for the passions. Posidonius' rather complicated theory of exhortation reflected the very widespread tendency in the hortatory tradition to equate or relate giving precepts and giving advice. Thus in the hortatory tradition the distinction between epideictic (praise and blame) and deliberative (giving advice) breaks down. The following types of letters were, at least sometimes, considered to be hortatory in antiquity: blame, reproach, reproof, consolation, praise, censure, encouragement, advice, and admonition.

Most of the types that I treat in this work are found in the handbooks under the pseudonyms of Demetrius and Libanius. They represent different traditions and often different points of view on types of letters but are nevertheless widely in agreement. The first gives twenty-one "types" of letters. This unknown author we refer to as Demetrius provides a brief description and sample letter for each type. Libanius has forty-one "styles" of letters. These are not model letters but nuggets of reasoning, often in the form of a rhetorical syllogism *(enthymeme),* which gives the gist of the kind of letter. The handbooks provide brief descriptions of ideal types for letters. Their authors realized that in practice the types would often be mixed and combined. Libanius even provides the "mixed letter" as his last type. Interestingly, it is a letter of praise and blame. The approaches of these handbooks to understanding letters allowed for the maximum flexibility which was required by the genre's occasional nature.

Libanius' handbook is entitled *Epistolimaioi Charaktēres* and is often translated, *Epistolary Styles.* But Libanius does not mean "style" either in the ancient or closely related modern sense. Libanius, for instance, does not mean the plain, elevated, elegant or forceful styles that the author who wrote the work *On Style* discusses. That author, also known in the tradition as Demetrius, advocates that the epistolary style should be a compound of the plain and graceful styles. Instead, Libanius' interest is in describing kinds or types of letters.

The epistolary handbook of Demetrius is much clearer than Libanius in its use of classificatory terminology:

> According to the theory that governs epistolary types *(typoi),* Heraclides, they can be composed from a great number of generic patterns *(eidē),* but arise from among those which always fit the particular circumstance [of the letter-writing situation]. . . . I have taken it upon myself, by means of certain generic categories *(ideai),* to organize and set forth both the number of distinctions between them and what they are, and have sketched a sample, as it were, of the arrangement of each kind *(genos taxeōs),* and have, in addition, individually set forth the fundamental logic *(logos)* for each of them. (1.1–11, Weichert; transl. modified from AET, p. 29)

Demetrius explains what he intends to do and the corresponding theory with clarity and concision. The theory of epistolary types requires that the writer compose according to generic patterns, which must fit the circumstances of the author's particular situation in writing. The "author's particular situation" would include his relationship to the recipient of the letter, the current status of the relationship, and the particular occasion for writing. Demetrius intends to describe and distinguish these types of letters, first by sketching a sample of how the type is arranged and, second, by explaining the logic of the type. Scholars have tended to suggest that Demetrius did not fulfill his task of describing genres of letters very well. What is missing from the model letters and their explanations has been more striking than what Demetrius actually says. Scholars have expected to find clear definitions in terms of formal features or characteristic *topoi.* The latter are commonplace topics and subjects of discussion.

Although Demetrius sometimes discusses or illustrates formal features and *topoi* that belong to the types, the essential elements of generic specification are a set of features that combine to outline a characteristic or recurrent social situation. The essential elements for the first two types Demetrius discusses are as follows:

The Friendly Type *(philikos)*
1. Two people separated
2. One person attempting to converse with the other
3. A relationship of friendship between the two
4. The writer attempting to maintain that relationship with the recipient

The Commending Type *(systatikos)*
1. Two people separated
2. One person attempting to converse with the other
3. An established positive social relationship between the two (e.g., friendship, family, patron-client)
4. The writer interceding on behalf of a third party in order to initiate a positive social relationship between the recipient and the third party

The first two elements are, of course, common to all letters. The other elements specify a typical social relationship in the culture and a customary action or activity which takes place within that social context. Together these are the essential elements by which not only Demetrius but also Libanius classify letters into types or genres *(typoi, genē, eidē).* Demetrius' examples show the arrangements of each kind *(genos taxeōs),* because they properly illustrate the relationship of these elements. The *logos* of each type refers to Demetrius' introductory comments which summarize the elements, make important distinctions, clarify possible confusions, and note exceptions to or developments of the type's logic.

The method of taxonomy found in the handbooks of Demetrius and Libanius is far from unique. It is an approach to classification employed widely in the rhetorical tradition. That tradition was virtually unanimous in defining the three *genē* of rhetoric by means of social contexts and characteristic activities of speech within those contexts: persuading a judge or jury of the justice or injustice of some act; persuading a civic assembly of the expediency or inexpediency of some future action; reinforcing the honorable on such occasions as weddings, birthdays, departures, and funerals.

Rhetoricians also divided *epideictic* into subgenres according to the same criteria of social situation and characteristic activity. The farewell speech to a departing traveler *(propemptikon),* for example, had three essential elements, someone departing, someone bidding farewell, and a relationship of friendship or affection between the two. This manner of classification is different from the division of literature by a combination of formal, structural, and stylistic criteria such as in the genres of epic, lyric, satire, elegy. The farewell speech must have the three essential elements to be a farewell speech. A structure together with certain styles and *topoi* were also typical of the farewell speech. The structure, styles and *topoi,* however, were variable and not unique to the *propemptic* genre. Speakers and writers employed the same topoi and styles in many different rhetorical genres. This is also true for types of letters. Each type of letter has certain essential elements in terms of social situations. It also has typical *topoi* and an appropriate style or styles, but the type may exist without the typical *topoi* and style. Furthermore, a type's style and *topoi* are often but not always employed in other kinds of letters.

The classification of speech and literature according to characteristic social occasion is understandable in light of the practice of tracing genres back to Homer. Grammarians and rhetoricians attempted to find models for every form of rhetoric and literature in Homer. Menander says:

> Among the many genres which the divine poet Homer taught us he did not neglect the genre *(eidos)* of monody. For he has conferred monodic speeches on Andromache, Priam, and Hecuba which are fitting for each of their characters, as if he wished to demonstrate to us that he was not ignorant of these things. We must therefore take our starting point from the poet and elaborate them as we understand the principle *(to theōrēma)* as the poet has handed it down to us. (434.11–18. Transl. by author)

This view of the Homeric heroes as exemplars of rhetorical skills was ancient (at least the fifth century B.C.E.) and became ubiquitous. Homer was the Bible for everything that was considered characteristic of genuinely Greek social life. The *theōrēma* which Homer provided for Menander was like Demetrius' and Libanius' descriptions of letter types. It was the bare sketch of a characteristic social occasion involving an appropriate act of speech. For both the epistolary theorists and Menander, this *theōrēma* was the fundamental generic logic that could be used as the basis for rhetorical elaboration through the employment of the principles of style and the selection and development of *topoi.*

A factor that was variable in some epistolary types and rhetorical genres was the social relationship between the speaker or writer and the audience. Certain genres had only one appropriate relationship, while others had two or more. The social relationship between speaker or writer and audience was one of the major criteria for the variation of style, structure, and *topoi.* In discussing the farewell speech *(propemptikon),* for example, Menander Rhetor says (395.4– 30) that the speech ought to be given in three different ways depending on the social relationship involved. If the speaker is socially superior to the traveler, he should give advice. If they are equals— that is, friends—the speaker should display his affection for the traveler. In the farewell speech of a social inferior to a superior, the speaker is to give praise to the traveler. The ancient speaker's culture required that he make use of an intricate social code. The modern interpreter of Greek and Roman literature who would understand the complexities of that literature must also grasp the social code. Epistolary theorists occasionally discuss the importance of the social relationship between writer and recipient. More often, this is only implicit in the logic of a type and confirmed by extant letters.

In sum, then, the concept of epistolary types provided the ancient writer with a taxonomy of letters according to typical actions performed in corresponding social contexts and occasions. The types in the handbooks give a sample, in barest outline, of form and language that is appropriate to the logic of the social code in a particular instance. The author, then, could elaborate, combine, and adapt this ideal according to the occasion in view, his purpose and his literary abilities. Rhetorical training provided the letter writer with techniques for the endless elaboration and development of the basic ideal captured in the handbook descriptions.

The modern student of ancient letters should understand both the limitations and the logic which the various types represent and the enormous flexibility in composition which they allow. In the following discussion of types that were important in early Christianity, I have tried to illustrate each type with letters that reflect a range of possibilities within the logic of the type. Some were written by people with very little education, others by those with the highest possible training. The illustrative letters also range from those of humble Egyptian tenant farmers to Roman emperors and formidable Christian bishops. My intention is that the reader may be able both to understand the ideal logic of the particular type and to sense the possibilities in its actual employment.

The order for my illustrative letters in each case is non-Christian papyrus examples, Christian papyrus examples, non-Christian "literary" letters, and Christian "literary" letters. I have tried to select examples that range over several centuries in order to provide some sense not only of changes in letter writing but also of the remarkable degree of conservation in the epistolary tradition. There are indeed changes in the tradition from the fourth century B.C.E. to the sixth century C.E., but its constancy and stability is most striking.

7

Letters of Friendship

Letters of friendship *(philikai)* constituted an important type of correspondence in antiquity. The theorists and educated writers of the Greek epistolary tradition assumed that the fundamental and proper function of the letter was the maintenance of friendship (e.g., Demetrius, *On Style* 225, 229, 231, 232). Ancient traditions and proverbs (e.g., Aristotle, *Nicomachean Ethics* 9.8.1168b, 6–8) asserted that friendship required the sharing of all things between socially and morally equal men, including affection and companionship. When being together was impossible, friendly letters *(philikai)* were said to provide a suitable substitute for actual companionship.

Demetrius gives the friendly letter as the first type in his handbook on letter writing.

> The friendly type, then, is one that seems to be written by a friend to a friend. But it is by no means (only) friends who write (in this manner). For frequently men in prominent positions are expected by some to write in a friendly manner to their inferiors and to others who are their equals, for example, to military commanders, viceroys, and governors. There are times, indeed, when they write to them without knowing them (personally). They do so, not because they are close friends and have (only) one choice (of how to write), but because they think that nobody will refuse them when they write in a friendly manner, but will rather submit and heed what they are writing. Nevertheless, this type of letter is called friendly as though it were written to a friend. It is as follows:

> Even though I have been separated from you for a long time, I suffer this in body only. For I can never forget you or the impeccable way we were reared together from childhood up. Knowing that I myself am genuinely concerned about your

affairs, and that I have worked unhesitatingly for what is most advantageous to you, I have assumed that you, too, have the same opinion of me, and will refuse me nothing. You will do well, therefore, to give close attention to the members of my household lest they need anything, to assist them in whatever they might need, and to write us about whatever you should choose.

Demetrius notes some important exceptions to the rule that friendly letters are for social equals. High officials often adopt the manner of friends in their letters even when writing to inferiors or people they do not know personally. Demetrius' rationale for this extension of the friendly letter is that writers use the friendly manner for persuading recipients to honor requests. Demetrius' handbook was probably written for letter writers in public service. His interest in this extension of the friendly letter is natural.

His model letter uses friendship as the basis for a request. It is not, however, a letter between people who lack personal acquaintance, as the reference to their shared childhood shows. Reminders concerning the foundation of friendship in past shared experiences are an important commonplace in friendly letters. Another commonplace is the writer's assertion that separation from his friend is only bodily; in mind and heart the two are united (cf. 1 Cor. 5:3; Col. 2:5; 1 Thess. 2:17). The ancient concept of friendship placed a stress on reciprocity in the giving of benefits, both in service and material goods. In Demetrius' example, the writer follows good form in reminding his friend of past benefits before he makes a request.

Libanius also gives a central place to friendly letters but in a different way. On the one hand, Libanius defines the friendly letter more strictly and traditionally than Demetrius: "The friendly genre is that in which we exhibit simple friendship only." By "simple friendship only" Libanius means that the friendly letter is to be used for the communication of the affection and concern that were traditional to letters of friendship. We might call this the letter of friendly affection. On the other hand, Libanius knows that friendship is more broadly tied to the epistolary tradition and he reflects this by using friendship as the imaginary social situation for eleven of his sample letters. In contrast to Demetrius, for example, the requesting letter in Libanius is a separate type that uses friendship as a warrant for the request: "As in the past I held your sacred friendship in high esteem, so now I expect to receive what I am requesting. . . . For it is right that genuine friends receive their requests" (54).

For Libanius, the friendly letter is just one kind of letter friends use.

As one would expect, then, Libanius' model letter consists only of some commonplaces traditional to letters of friendship. The sample expresses the central idea of the friendly letter; friends share in each other's minds through letters when they are physically separated.

> The friendly letter. Since I have many sterling letter carriers available, I am eager to address your intelligent mind. For it is a holy thing to honor genuine friends when they are present, and to speak to them when they are absent.

In Aristotle's ideal theory of the state, citizenship is coextensive with friendship. Aristotle's goal was to eliminate the strife and competition among the factions of friends that had dominated Greek politics. Even with Aristotle's broadening, however, true friendship and citizenship were denied to women, slaves, and resident noncitizens. Both Greek and Roman friendship had socially exclusive upper-class roots. It is not surprising, then, that good examples of friendly letters increase as the social status of the writers increase. Friendly letters dominate the collections of many highly placed authors, but are not common among the papyri. Nevertheless, the letter of friendship was so important to the epistolary tradition that its commonplaces and phraseology widely influenced virtually all levels and types of letter writing.

The New Testament

Although there are no letters of friendship in the New Testament, some letters employ commonplaces and language from the friendly letter tradition. The commonplace "absent in body but present in spirit" occurs in 2 Cor. 5:3; 10:1–2 (?); Col. 2:5; and 1 Thess. 2:17. The theme of "longing to be with the loved one" appears in 2 Cor. 1:16; 1 Thess. 3:6–10; Philemon 22; 2 John 12; 3 John 14. The following commonplaces of the friendly letter may also possibly appear as follows: "yearning for the loved one," Phil. 1:7–8; "sharing in one another's feelings," Phil. 2:17–18; "letter writing as a conversation," 1 Cor. 10:15.

Claudius to Sarapion

Papyrus letters of friendship are often short notes like the letter of Claudius to Sarapion, expressing affection and offering friendly service. Both men were probably high officials in the Roman administration of Egypt. The letter was written by a secretary except for the closing prayer and farewell, which are in another hand, almost certainly that of Claudius himself. This practice was like adding a signature to a typed letter. The apostle Paul does the same at the close of some letters in order to provide a personal touch: "I, Paul, write this greeting with my own hand" (1 Cor. 16:21; see also Gal. 6:11; Col. 4:18; Philemon 19; cf. Rom. 16:22).

Upper Egypt   Early second century C.E.
*SB*4, 7335
Transl. by author

Claudius Agathas Daimon to most beloved Sarapion, greetings. Since I am going to Thebes, I salute you dearest, sweetest Sarapion and I exhort you also to do the same thing. If you need anything from Thebes, I encourage you to write to me, dearest, and it shall be done. *(2nd hand)* I pray for your health continually together with that of your children. Farewell. *(Verso)* To Sarapion *kosmētēs* of Hermopolis.

Chairas to Dionysius

This friendly letter is addressed to a physician. The author's placement of a request for a medical recipe within the context of his friendship with the doctor is reminiscent of Demetrius' treatment of the friendly letter. Three commonplaces of the friendly letter tradition appear at the beginning. First, Chairas describes his delight at receiving a letter from Dionysius and compares the experience to the feeling of being at home. Descriptions of the wonderful effects caused by reading a friend's letter are quite common. Second, Chairas adds the commonplace that friends need not verbally express their thanks (or praise). A friend is a second self. Friends know each other's minds. Third, the writer expresses his desire to reciprocate Dionysius' affection.

Oxyrhynchus or Hermopolis, Egypt   August 29, 58 C.E.
P.Merton 12
Transl. by author

Chairas to his dearest Dionysius, many greetings and continual health. I was as much delighted at receiving a letter from you as if I had indeed been in my native place; for apart from that we have nothing. I may dispense with writing to you with a great show of thanks; for it is to those who are not friends that we must give thanks in words. I trust that I may maintain myself in some degree of serenity and be able, if not to give you an equivalent, at least to show some small return for your affection towards me. You sent me two prescription-copies, one of the Archagathian, the other of the caustic plaster. The Archagathian is rightly compounded, but the caustic does not include the relative weight of resin. Please tell me of a strong caustic which can safely be used to cauterize the soles (of the feet); for I am in urgent need. As to the dry (?) plaster, you wrote that there are two kinds. Send me the prescription for the resolvent kind; for the four-drug plaster is also dry (?). This letter is sealed with this (?). Farewell and remember what I have said. Year 5 of Nero the lord, month of Germanicus 1. *(Address)* To Dionysius, physician.

To Isidorus

The name of the person who sent the following letter to Isidorus has been lost. The letter illustrates the frequently encountered difficulty of distinguishing friendly from family letters among the Egyptian papyri. The writer calls Isidorus his brother but that is the only possible indication of a family relationship. He also uses language of affection traditional to friendship. The word translated as "friend," however, can also be translated more neutrally as "dear" or "beloved." Since brother is often used loosely for friends it is impossible to determine the exact relationship with certainty. At any rate, it makes an excellent example of a friendly letter which compares well with both Demetrius' and Libanius' model letters. The idea that letters provide a surrogate for seeing or speaking with a friend is an important commonplace. Seneca tells Lucilius that, "I prefer that my letters should be just what my conversation would be if you and I were sitting in one another's company or taking walks together, . . . spontaneous and easy" (*Letter* 75.1), and "I never receive a letter from you without being in your company forthwith" (*Letter* 40.1).

Philadelphia, Egypt   Late second century c.e.
ZPE 22(1976): 51
Transl. by author

. . . to Isidorus, my brother, greetings. Upon reaching Antinoöpolis, I received your letter, through which I experienced the feeling of seeing you. I therefore urge you to keep writing continually, for in this way our friendship will be increased. When I am slow to write to you, this happens easily because I am not able to find anyone traveling your way. Write to me about any need you might have since you know that I will comply without delay. If you write me a letter, send it to my friend Hermes at the house of Artemis so that he may deliver it to me. Hermes himself and his sister Tausiris send you many greetings. Farewell. *(Verso)* Deliver to my friend Isidorus in Philadelphia from [. . .]

Apollonius to Dioscurides

The letter from Apollonius to Dioscurides is a good papyrus illustration of the extension of friendship language to official superior/subordinate relationships which Demetrius discusses. Apollonius addresses Dioscurides as "friend" and yet writes to him in the body of the letter as to a subordinate. Apollonius is almost certainly a tax collector. Dioscurides and Polydas, his field men, have for some reason not collected the taxes in their districts. Instead of the rebuke that one would expect, Apollonius approaches his subordinate as a friend.

Egypt   Second century C.E.
Transl. by J. D. Thomas, *P.Oxy.* 2861

Apollonius to his very dear friend Dioscurides greeting. As I asked you when I saw you to proceed vigorously with the collection of the accounts on your list, so now I ask you still more to apply yourself to the collection with urgency of the substantial (?) accounts, since we have been compelled to pay everything into the bank. I have found too that Polydas has collected nothing and I have remained here of necessity. Farewell. *(Address)* To Dioscurides from Apollonius his friend.

Cicero to Curio

Cicero's letter to Scribonius Curio illustrates the friendly letter from the highest levels of Roman society. Curio would later prove himself false to his friendship with Cicero and join Caesar's party. It was men from this level of society who ruled. Politics is therefore inseparable from friendship. Cicero gives treatment to one of the commonplaces of the friendly letter when he devotes the first part to a lighthearted defense against the charge of not reciprocating Curio's letters. Writers would often feign hurt feelings at not receiving letters promptly or in the right quantity. Such grousing was itself considered to be a show of affection. Here Cicero turns the charge against Curio. Cicero's lament at Curio's absence and rejoicing at his fortune are also commonplaces. He goes on to give his younger friend some advice which seems to be simple moral exhortation: "Keep on perfecting the good character which you have already developed." It is well to remember, however, that Curio was one of the bright young hopes of Cicero's political faction. Cicero is hinting at Curio's indebtedness to him.

Rome   53 B.C.E.
Transl. by W. G. Williams, *Cicero: Letters
    to His Friends* 2.1 (LCL)

M. Cicero to C. Scribonius Curio. Though I am sorry you should have suspected me on the score of "neglect," still I am more pleased that you missed my attentions than put out that you should accuse me of any remissness, especially since in so far as your charge went, I was in no sense to blame, while in so far as you implied that you longed for a letter from me, you openly avowed an affection for me, which, well as I knew it before, is none the less delightful and desirable. As a matter of fact I have not let a single carrier pass, if I thought he would reach you, without giving him a letter for you. Come now, who so indefatigable a correspondent as I? As for you, I have only had two or three letters from you at the most, and those very short ones. Therefore if you judge me harshly, I shall find you guilty on the same charge; if you don't want me to do so, you will have to be lenient with me. But no more about correspondence; I am not afraid of failing to give you your fill of letters, especially if you show a proper appreciation of my efforts in that line.

I have grieved at your long absence from among us, because I have not been able to enjoy your most agreeable society, but at the same time I rejoice that while absent you have attained all your objects with the greatest honour to yourself, and that in all your affairs fortune has answered my prayers. There is a little piece of advice which my extraordinary affection for you compels me to offer you. So much is expected of your courage, or, it may be of your capacity, that I do not hesitate to beg and beseech you to return to us in such a frame of mind as to be able to uphold and justify all the expectations you have excited. And while it is true that no forgetfulness will ever efface the memory of what you have done for me, I beg you to remember that, whatever enhancements of fortune or honour may accrue to you in the future, you could never have secured them, had you not in the old days of your boyhood hearkened to the advice given you in all sincerity and affection by myself. And that is why your feelings towards me should be such, that, burdened as I am with the increasing weight of years, I should find repose in your love and in your youth.

Julian to Iamblichus

The following is an attempt to imagine a letter of friendship from someone (perhaps the emperor Julian) to the philosopher Iamblichus. What the author produced was an extravagant parody of a friendly letter based upon a rhetorical elaboration of the commonplace, "joy at the experience of receiving a friend's letter." Since it is a parody it highlights many characteristics of the friendly letter for us by exaggeration.

Provenance unknown   Fourth century C.E.
Transl. by W. C. Wright, *Works of the*
  Emperor Julian, Letter 77 (LCL)

"Thou hast come! Well hast thou done!" You have indeed come, even though absent, by means of your letter—"And I was yearning for thee, and thou didst set ablaze my heart, already aflame with longing for thee." Nay, I neither refuse the love-philtre nor do I ever leave you at all, but with my soul I behold you as though you were present, and am with you when absent and nothing is enough to quench my insatiate desire. Moreover, you also never slacken, but without ceasing you benefit those who are present with you and by your letters not only cheer but even heal those who are absent. At any rate, when someone not long ago gave me the news that a friend had come and brought letters from you, it happened that for three days I had been suffering from a disorder of the stomach, and in fact I was in acute physical pain, so that I was not even free from fever. But, as I said, when I was told that the person who had the letters was at my door I jumped up like one possessed, who has lost control of himself, and rushed out before what I wanted could arrive. And the moment that I merely took the letter in my hands, I swear by the very gods and by the love that burns in me for you, that instant my pains forsook me and at once the fever let me go, as though it were abashed by some manifest saving presence. But when I broke the seal and read the letter, can you imagine what feelings took possession of my soul.
. . . But how could I describe my other sensations when first I

read the letter, or how could I find adequate words to betray my own passion? How often did I hark back from the middle to the beginning? . . . How often I held the letter to my lips, as mothers embrace their children, how often I kissed it with those lips as though I were embracing my dearest sweetheart, how often I invoked and kissed and held to my eyes even the superscription which had been signed by your own hand as though by a clear cut seal, and how I clung to the imprint of the letters as I should to the fingers of that sacred right hand of yours! I too "wish thee joy in full measure," as fair Sappho says, and not only "for just so long as we have been parted from one another," but may you rejoice evermore, and write to me and remember me with kindly thoughts. For no time shall ever pass by me in which I shall forget you, in any place, at any hour, in any word I speak. "But if ever Zeus permits me to return to my native land," and once more I humbly approach that sacred hearth of yours, do not spare me hereafter as you would a runaway, but fetter me, if you will, to your own beloved dwelling. . . . I would gladly fasten myself to your tunic, my noble friend, so that I might never for a moment leave your side but be with you always and closely attached to you wherever you are, like those two-bodied beings invented in the myths. Unless, indeed, in this case also the myths, though they tell us the story in jest, are describing in enigmatical words an extraordinary sort of friendship and by that close tie of a common being express the kinship of soul in both beings.

Epicurus to a Child

The various philosophical schools developed their own theories of friendship. Of all the sects, the Epicureans held friendship to be most central. For them friendship was the key to human happiness and freedom. Epicurean friendship was set apart from normal friendship by its apolitical and egalitarian characteristics. Only fragments of Epicurus' friendly letters have survived but in them a picture of Epicurean friendship is visible. Like the earliest Christians, Epicurus modified the standard opening greetings in order to express his own philosophical perspective: Instead of "greetings" he is said to have used "be well," "prosper," or "live well." The following letter to a child illustrates Epicurus' extension of friendship to include both sexes and all ages. The letter was discovered among a library of Epicurean writings during the excavations of

Herculaneum, one of the cities destroyed by the eruption of Mt. Vesuvius in 79 C.E.

Lampsacus   Third century B.C.E.
Text from Hermann Usener,
    Epicurea, p. 154
Transl. by author

We have arrived at Lampsacus in good health, Pythocles, Hermarchus, Ctesippus, and I. There we found Themista and the rest of our friends in good health. I hope that you also are in good health and your mother and that you are always obedient to your father and Matro, as you have been. For you can be sure that the reason why both I and all the rest love you greatly is that you always obey them.

Basil to Jovinus

Letters of friendship between Christians in elite circles appear in remarkable numbers in the fourth and fifth centuries A.D. The following letter from Basil, bishop of Caesarea in Cappadocia, to Jovinus, a count of the empire, eloquently expresses the idea of the letter as a surrogate for a friend's personal presence: The letter as an image of the writer's soul is a motif which is developed primarily in extant Christian letter writers of the late fourth and fifth centuries. Note also the commonplace of the letter as a consolation for a friend's absence; a consolation of which Basil claims need because he has been unable to visit Jovinus. Basil's letter is typical of letters from the later period but is unlike earlier Christian letters in lacking expansive greetings, prayers, and salutations.

Caesarea, Cappadocia   374 C.E.
Transl. by R. J. Deferrari, *Saint Basil: The
    Letters* 2.419–421 (LCL)

I saw your soul in your letter. For truly no painter can grasp so accurately the characteristics of the body as words can portray the secrets of the soul. For when I read your letter, its words adequately delineated to us the soundness of your character, the genuineness of your worth, and the integrity of your mind in everything; and so it brought to us great consolation for your absence. Therefore do not leave off availing yourself of any excuse that arises from time to time for writing me and for conferring on me the boon of this too long interrupted conversation; for our bodily weakness causes us now to despair of a personal interview. How serious an illness it is will be explained to you by our most God-beloved bishop Amphilochius, who possesses both the knowledge by reason of having been much with us, and the ability to set forth in speech whatever he has seen. And I wish my difficulties to be known for no other object than your pardon in the future, that we may not be condemned for indifference if we do fail to pay you the visit. And yet there is not so much need of a defence as of some consolation to me for my loss therein. For if it had been possible for me to be with your August Reverence, I should have considered this as worth far more to me than the objects for which others earnestly strive.

Synesius to Pylaemenes

In the friendly letters of Synesius, bishop of Cyrene, Platonic eros is explicitly a model for his friendship with Pylaemenes and others. Letter 129 begins with the following lines: "In Plato we see Socrates already advanced in years seeking out his loves. 'Do not be surprised,' he says to them, 'if after having given myself up to love with difficulty, I renounce it also with difficulty.' " He begins Letter 140 by saying: "Of loves there are some which have earthly and human origins. These are detestable and ephemeral, measured by the presence of the object alone, and even then with difficulty. But there are others over which Divinity presides, and according to the divine utterance of Plato, he fuses those who love one another by his art, so that from being two they become one." These quotations well serve as commentary on Letter 152 and illustrate the importance of the classical tradition to later Christian epistolography.

Cyrene   Late fourth or early fifth century c.e.
Transl. by Augustine Fitzgerald, *The*
    Letters of Synesius of Cyrene, p. 249

Believe me that I embrace Pylaemenes, very soul and very soul. Words fail me wherewith I may pour out the fullness of my heart's desire, or rather I cannot explain, even to myself, the nature of the sentiments that I feel for you. But there was one man at least who was extraordinary in all knowledge of Love. That was Plato the Athenian, the son of Ariston, so happy in discovering, and pleasant in describing the nature of the lover and also his desires in regard to the beloved. It is he, therefore, who shall discover and describe for me. The man who loves, he said, would fain be melted by the art of Hephaestus, and so completely united with the beloved object, that two would become one.

Jerome to Florentius

Writers also gave specifically Christian turns to the motifs and topics of the friendly letter. Jerome, the great scholar and fanatical exponent of the ascetic movement, wrote Letter 5 to Florentius from his monastic hideaway in the Syrian desert. This opening to a friendly letter of request displays Jerome's considerable rhetorical abilities as he develops commonplaces of friendship in a Christian way.

Syria 374 C.E.
Transl. by W. H. Fremantle, *Principal*
 Works of Jerome (NPNF), p. 7

Your letter, dear friend, finds me dwelling in that quarter of the desert which is nearest to Syria and the Saracens. And the reading of it rekindles in my mind so keen a desire to set out for Jerusalem that I am almost ready to violate my monastic vow in order to gratify my affection. Wishing to do the best I can, as I cannot come in person I send you a letter instead; and thus, though absent in the body, I come to you in love and in spirit. For my earnest prayer is that our infant friendship, firmly cemented as it is in Christ, may never be rent asunder by time or distance. We ought rather to strengthen the bond by an interchange of letters. Let these pass between us, meet each other on the way, and converse with us. Affection will not lose much if it keeps up an intercourse of this kind.

Additional Examples of Friendly Letters

For non-Christian examples see: *P.Oxy.* 1664, 3057; fragments of Epicurus, *To Colotes, To Idomenus;* Cicero's *Letters to Atticus* and *Letters to Friends* (many of which are friendly letters, e.g., *To Friends* 2.1, 2); *Socratics* 25, 31; Diogenes of Oenoanda, Frag. 51 (Chilton); Libanius, *Letters* 52, 53, 94, 258, 481, 760, 1028, 1450; Apollonius of Tyana, *Letter* 49. For Christian examples see: Basil, *Letters* 11, 12, 13, 19, 20, 57, 91, 133, 163; Gregory of Nyssa, *Letters* 7, 14; Gregory of Nazianzus, *Letters* 49, 64, 66, 73, 225; John Chrysostom, *Letters* 36, 49, 58; Synesius, *Letters* 48, 70, 71, 97, 129, 134, 139, 140, 146, 149, 151–153, 159; Ambrose, *Letter* 197; Augustine, *Letters* 42, 58; Jerome, *Letters* 5, 7; Paulinus of Nola, *Letter* 20.

8

Family Letters

The family or household letter was never recognized as a type by the ancient theorists. In fact, very many of the types were customarily employed in correspondence between members of the household. Yet the epistolary theorists could have isolated the family letter as a type analogous to the friendly letter: A letter for maintaining the affection and social relationships of the household. The Greek epistolographic tradition was too closely tied to the traditionally segregated literate culture of free adult males, i.e., friendship, for that to happen. The papyri from Egypt have shown the enormous lacunae that would be left in our picture of letter writing if we were to follow the epistolary theorists at this point.

Family letters written by those at the top of the social pyramid often allow a fairly clear picture of the household with its own hierarchy of blood relatives, servants, and slaves. The cities of the empire were predominantly Greek and Roman in culture and family structure. Outside of the cities, however, the country towns and villages were marked by seemingly endless variation in custom and local cultures, for instance that of the Jews in Galilee or the native Egyptians in Egypt. The family structure and relationships of letter writers in the Egyptian papyri are often far from clear, even if those involved write in Greek and have Greek names. Most of these people write about matters pertaining to the economic activities of the household and attempt to maintain the bonds of community and affection among blood relatives by letter. Characteristically, the writer of a family letter has been forced to leave home because of economic necessity, the service of government, or the illness of a relative. The traveler then writes back reporting about the situation and expressing his affection for the family and anxiety over separation.

Achillion to Hieracapollon

The letter from Achillion to Hieracapollon is typical of many familial letters from Egypt; it is brief, formal and does little beyond making an expression of familial contact and concern. The author calls Hieracapollon his brother and reports that he is sending for his sister and their son Dionysius. One of the persistently bothersome problems in interpreting papyrus letters is the Egyptian practice of using family titles for others than those to whom they literally apply. Older men called younger men "son." Husbands and wives constantly called each other "sister" and "brother"; "father" or "mother" could refer to any older man or woman. Thus we do not know if Hieracapollon was Achillion's actual brother. The reference to "our son," however, probably shows that Achillion and his "sister" were husband and wife. The word "sister" could be more than a title of affection since brothers and sisters sometimes married in Egypt. The salutation and request for news about health is customary language for such letters. The expressions about doing a favor and seeing one another face to face are common epistolary clichés or formulas, as is the concluding prayer for health.

Oxyrhynchus, Egypt   Third century c.e.
Transl. by P. J. Parsons, *P.Oxy.* 3067

Achillion to Hieracapollon his brother, greetings. Since I am in process of sending for my sister, I send you a letter, as in duty bound, by the hands of those whom I have dispatched for this purpose: a letter first to salute you and my sister and our son Dionysius; secondly to exhort you to write to me about your health and about your requirements here. Do this, and you will be doing me a favour; we shall have the impression, through our letters, of seeing one another face to face. *(2nd hand)* I pray for your health. *(Address)* To Hieracapollon his brother *(3rd hand)* from Achillion, strategus of the Marmarica.

Heraklas to Horos and Tachonis

The following letter is dated to the rule of Augustus (27 b.c.e.–14 c.e.). A man who is on military duty writes to his son and most probably his wife. He expresses his concern about some threat to his son (illness?) and then launches into instructions about financial matters in the way so typical of familial papyri.

Provenance unknown   Reign of Augustus
Ed. *BJRL* 51: 151–154
Transl. by G. H. R. Horsley, *NDIEC*
   (1981), p. 52

Heraklas to Horos and Tachonis, greetings and good health. Don't worry about us. Since we've been on military duty we have been sailing in the boat for eight days. With the gods' will in three days we shall be on shipboard. As for the child keep an eye on him as you would an oil lamp, since I am worried about you. If Apollo's son comes to you about what remains, indicate [pretend?] to him that it is coming with haste by [to?] Ptollas along with my accounts. I said that I kept an eye on [. . .] to give to the fuller concerning [. . .] least. I know about the weaver's 4 drachmai [. . .] 20 drachmai for the sake of the other weaver the [. . .] and indicate that I am coming quickly. Farewell—year of Caesar Augustus. Choiak 13 (= 9 December). *(Verso)* [. . .] and to Horos his son.

Aurelius Dius to His Father

Aurelius Dius is a student away at school who writes home to his father. Perhaps a third of the papyrus family letters have some kind of wish for well-being (see letter of Heraklas above) or "prayer" after the initial salutation. In the second and third centuries C.E. this is frequently expressed, as by Aurelius Dius, in an obeisance formula. (Compare Paul in 1 Thess. 1:2: "We always give thanks to God for all of you, constantly making mention of you in our prayers"; cf. 3 John 2.) Like Paul in Romans 16 and numerous family letters from the mid-first century B.C.E. onward, Aurelius salutes several other people at the end of his letter. These may all be members of his household. Notice that he salutes a certain Melanus and another Horion (not his real father) as father.

Oxyrhynchus, Egypt   Third century C.E.
P.Oxy. 1296
Transl. by A. S. Hunt and C. C. Edgar,
   Select Papyri (LCL), no. 137

Aurelius Dius to Aurelius Horion, my sweetest father, many greetings. I make supplication for you every day before the gods of this place. Now do not be uneasy, father, about my studies; I am working hard and taking relaxation; I shall do finely. I salute my mother Tamiea and my sister Tnepherous and my sister Philous, I salute also my brother Patermouthis and my sister Thermouthis, I salute also my brother Heracl [. . .] and my brother Kollouchis, I salute my father Melanus and my mother Timpesouris and her son. Gaia salutes you all, my father Horion and Thermouthis salute you all. I pray for your health, father. *(Address)* Deliver to Aurelius Horion from his son Dius.

Besas to His Mother

In the following letter, a Christian boy wrote in a child's handwriting to his mother. The expression "above all I pray for your health" occurs among the papyri from the first century c.e. onward. The boy's Christianized prayer mentions God the Father and the Holy Spirit but not Christ. Besas has either studied the letters of Paul or picked up a local Christian tradition since the soul, body, and spirit expression is based on 1 Thess. 5:23. The Spirit is called Comforter in the Gospel of John.

Provenance unknown   Third century c.e.
P.Harr. 107
Transl. by author

To my most precious mother, from Besas, many greetings in God. Before all I pray to our Father, the God of truth, and to the Spirit who is the Comforter that he may guard you in soul, body, and spirit, and give health to your body, cheerfulness to your spirit, and eternal life to your soul. If you find someone coming my direction, do not hesitate to write me a letter concerning your health so that I might hear and rejoice. Do not neglect to send me a cloak for the Easter holiday and send my brother to me. I salute my father and my brothers. I pray that all of you might have continual good health.

Cicero to His Family

The following letter was written by Cicero at Thessalonica on October the fifth, 58 b.c.e., and sent to his wife Terentia and his family in Rome. At the time, Cicero was in exile, having been declared an outlaw and having had his property confiscated. Letters such as Cicero's are usually set in the sharpest contrast to the papyrus letters. It is well to remember, however, that Cicero's are not literary pieces but occasional letters written in the midst of everyday life. Letters written by people from the upper levels of Hellenistic and Roman society are understandably different from the typical papyrus letters of barely literate or illiterate people. People like Cicero lived lives of much greater complexity with sophisticated literary and linguistic abilities cultivated through rhetorical and philosophical training. It is not surprising that their letters are also much more articulate and complex. They can also be considerably longer than most papyrus letters (but also see Cicero, *To Friends* 14.8–13, which are papyrus-like in length and other respects). Finally, the reader should keep in mind that Cicero writes in Latin and follows certain stylistic conventions unique to Latin letters.

Thessalonica   58 B.C.E.
Transl. by W. G. Williams, *Cicero: Letters*
     to His Friends 14.2 (LCL)

Cicero to his own Terentia, Tullia, and Cicero. You must never think that I write longer letters to anybody unless somebody has written to me at unusual length, and I think it my duty to answer him. For nothing I find greater difficulty in doing. But to you and our darling Tullia I cannot write without a flood of tears. I see that both of you are utterly wretched, you, whom I have always wished to be completely happy—a happiness it was my duty to have secured, and I should have secured it, had I not been so timorous.

For our friend Piso I have a profound affection, and it is no more than he deserves. I have done my best to urge him on by letter, and have thanked him as I was bound to do. I gather that you have hopes of the new tribunes of the plebs. On that we may rely, if we can rely on Pompey's friendliness; and yet I have my fears of Crassus. As for yourself, I see that you are acting in every respect most courageously and lovingly, nor does it surprise me; but what saddens me is the nature of a calamity in which my own miseries can only be alleviated at the cost of such miseries to you. For that most obliging of men, P. Valerius, had described in a letter to me (and I wept bitterly as I read it) how you were haled from the temple of Vesta to the Valerian Office. Alas, light of my life, for whom I yearn, to whom all used to look for help, to think that now, Terentia mine, you are thus harassed, thus laid low in tears and unseemly humiliation! And to think that it is all my fault, who have saved others to perish myself!

I implore you, my darling, as far as expense is concerned, to let others, who can if they only will, bear the burden, and do not, as you love me, tax that indifferent health of yours. Day and night you are ever before my eyes. I see you taking upon yourself all our troubles, and I fear it is too much for you. But I also see that everything depends upon you; and for that reason, in order that we may succeed in what you are hoping and striving for, obey the dictates of health.

I know not to whom I should write, unless it is to those who write to me, or to those about whom you and Tullia say anything in your letters to me. Since that is your wish, I am not going farther away; but I should like you to send me a letter as often as possible, especially if we have any better foundation for our hopes. Good-bye, you dear ones for whom I long, good-bye. Thessalonica, Oct. 5th.

9

Letters of Praise
and Blame

Letters of Praise (*epainetikai*)

Praising and blaming were fundamental activities through which the social construction of the ancient world was maintained. Praise legitimated and effected social structures and constructions of reality. The myriads of inscriptions and monuments, for example, which decorated the cities of the empire, praised a class of men who were destined by wealth and noble birth to be benefactors. Whatever one praised, whether it be the character of a friend, the cosmic rhythms of nature, or the virtues of Rome, that thing or person was affirmed, legitimated, and objectified. In a society where there is deep agreement about "the way things ought to be," those who give praise and blame work to locate each person and thing in their proper place by bestowing honor and causing shame. It was honorable for a noble person to be generous. It was dishonorable for a woman to have power over a free man. Some philosophical groups and Christians might challenge the accepted structure of honorable and dishonorable behavior, but they did not challenge the system of honor itself or the process of praise and blame through which the system was sustained.

Letters of praise and blame, then, are perhaps the most basic and most ideal of the types. Praise and/or blame is used in virtually every type of letter that the theorists isolated. The ancients defined one of the three departments of rhetoric, *epideictic* (see p. 51), as the speech of praise and blame that demonstrated the honorable and shameful. Some also defined exhortation as the praise and blame of habits of behavior. Moralists argued that praise and blame were harmful unless employed as a kind of exhortation. Praise of persons, then, was sometimes viewed as a type of exhortation (see chapter 10 on letters of exhortation).

Quintilian (*Education of the Orator* 3.7.29ff.) and other rhetorical theorists pointed out that deliberative and epideictic rhetoric were akin since the speaker advised the same things in the former that he praised in the latter. The list of the things that speakers and writers praised was extremely long. Synesius answered Dio Chrysostom's *Encomium of Hair* with wit in his *Encomium of Baldness.* Greek culture knew Homer as the one who praised everything praiseworthy in the world. But from the Sophists and Plato onward, philosophers tried to modify the map of what was praiseworthy. The Christians offered an even more radically revised map that included traditions of what was praiseworthy from the culture of Judaism.

The epistolary theorists understood the letter of praise (*epainetikē*) as a letter whose purpose was to praise a person rather than a place or a thing. Demetrius highlights the hortatory function of praise (cf. Seneca, *Letter* 94.39).

> It is the praising type when we encourage someone and express our approval of what he has done or has proposed to do, in the following manner:
>
> I had earlier shared in your excellent character through the letters that you wrote; now I approve of what you have done and encourage you, for it will be profitable to us both.

Demetrius indicates that the object of praise is a person's actions while Libanius speaks of a person's outstanding virtue. Both actions and virtue, i.e., habits of behavior, are interrelated. In his letter, Demetrius prefaces his praise of the recipient's actions with an acknowledgment of his excellent character. The author of the *Epistolary Types* reveals his knowledge of the hortatory tradition by explicitly claiming that the function of praise is "to encourage." This latter word, *parakaleō*, is frequently used in the New Testament and other early Christian literature as a hortatory term and translated as "encourage," "exhort," or "beseech." In Demetrius' formulation, encouragement follows from "approval" (*apodechomai*). In fact, letters of praise were sometimes called letters of "approval" (e.g., Eusebius, *History of the Church* 4.23.5, 9; mistranslated as "welcome" in the LCL). Finally, Demetrius implies some close but unspecified relationship between writer and recipient. The writer uses the commonplace from the friendly letter of sharing in the letter writer's character and says that the recipient's actions will be profitable for both.

Libanius displays no interest in praise as exhortation. Instead, he is concerned to distinguish praise from *encomium.* This topic was widely discussed by rhetoricians. Some did not distinguish the two, while others went to great lengths to do so (e.g., Alexander, son of Numenius, in Spengel 3.1–2; also Hermogenes, Spengel 2.25; and Aristides, Spengel 2.505, 506). Praise, blame, and encomium were also discussed and taught in the elementary rhetorical exercises *(progymnasmata)*. Libanius' distinction is significant for defining the letter of praise. Although the two terms could be used interchangeably in a general sense, "encomium" was also the name for an old and established epideictic genre in which a person or thing was praised. The person or thing was praised according to a rather comprehensive and systematic set of standard topics. The major topic headings for the encomium of a person were family, birth, nature, nurture, education, and accomplishments. These were each in turn divided into several subheadings in the typical encomium. There are encomiastic letters which employ these commonplaces. Libanius wants to distinguish sharply the letter of praise from encomiastic letters. Letters of praise are about one thing.

> The praising style is that in which we praise someone eminent in virtue. We should recognize that praise differs from an encomium. For praise is laudatory speech praising one thing, but an encomium is encomiastic speech embracing many things in itself. Therefore, the letter that praises one thing is called laudatory, and that which praises many features is called encomiastic:

> The letter of praise. I praise and honor you for your astuteness and surpassing intelligence. For it is fitting, not only to praise extraordinary men, but also to honor them.

Libanius' restriction of praise to one thing should probably not be taken too literally. The important point seems to be the distinction between simple letters of praise which honor a person on a certain occasion or for a specific achievement and encomiastic letters which praise the person in a more comprehensive way. That is the sort of distinction which is useful in view of extant letters of praise.

The fundamental elements of the praising letter are as follows:

1. The writer most often has a relationship of inferiority or equality with the recipient.
2. The writer honors and sometimes also encourages the recipient by praising a limited number of the recipient's actions as manifestations of character traits.

Praise and blame were often mixed. Moralists and philosophers argued for balance in their use. Too much praise became flattery and too much blame became harmful instead of helpful. Plutarch, in his *How to Tell a Flatterer from a Friend,* writes, "Like any other medicine, frankness if not applied at the appropriate time, only causes useless pain and trouble . . . for people are injured not only by untimely praise but also by untimely blame" (66B). Furthermore, the person who has received proper and timely praise has been opened to the acceptance of blame as useful criticism (50B). Dio Chrysostom tells the people of Tarsus that they can expect little praise from him, since censure and rebuke which expose sin are more helpful and are the task of the Cynic philosopher (*Oration* 33.12). But Dio also advocates that blame be applied with a gentle touch. Moralists compared the practice of mixing praise and blame to that of mixing foul-tasting medicine with honey. Theodoret attempted a Christian adaptation of the rules of praise which he justified through scripture (*Letter* 39, Sakkelion collection).

Pure letters of praise are uncommon among the papyri except in situations where clients and subordinates praise superiors. These letters only appear in significant numbers in the late fourth and fifth centuries. Letters of blame and letters mixing praise with blame are common throughout the range of papyrus letters. Letters of praise are prominent in several different social contexts, e.g., client-patron, friendship, philosophical groups, among the literarily transmitted letters. The same is also true of blame and mixed letters. Approval and disapproval are so basic to human interaction that elements of praise and blame are components of nearly every type of letter. The letter of thanks, for example, was considered praise of a person for a specific benefaction.

The New Testament

Although no pure letters of praise exist in the New Testament, Paul makes a significant use of praise in certain parts of his letters. He characteristically includes a word of praise for the recipients in his thanksgiving (e.g., Rom. 1:8; 1 Thess. 1:3; 2 Thess. 1:3–4; Philemon 1–4). In 1 Corinthians 11, Paul balances praise and blame in the service of giving advice (cf. 11:2, 17, 22). Chapter 13 of the same letter is comparable to passages in Greco-Roman literature that praise virtues. Six of the seven letters in Revelation 2 and 3 (those to Ephesus, Smyrna, Pergamum, Thyatira, Sardis, and Philadelphia) mix praise with something else such as blaming, threatening, consolation, or promising. In good epistolary form they begin with praise and then turn to blaming or threatening.

Fronto to Marcus Aurelius

Fronto, the teacher of rhetoric and orator, wrote the following letter to Marcus Aurelius a few years after Marcus became Caesar. Fronto had been his tutor after the adoption of the future emperor by Hadrian in 138. The orator first praises Marcus for his ability to unite friends and then turns the praise into an exhortation for Marcus to keep harmony among his devotees. As in Demetrius' model letter and 1 Corinthians 11, praise is used in the service of advice, the approval of a certain behavior. The letter opens with Fronto comparing Marcus to Orpheus, whose image appeared on the coins of Marcus from Alexandria. The letter closes with a rhetorically extravagant protestation of Fronto's love for Marcus.

Italy (?)   140–143 C.E.
Transl. by C. R. Haines, *Correspondence of
M. C. Fronto, Ad M. Caes.* 4.1 (LCL)

Fronto to my Lord. Since I know how anxious you are. ... Sheep and doves with wolves and eagles followed the singer, regardless of ambushes and talons and teeth. This legend rightly interpreted surely signifies this, that Orpheus was a man of matchless genius and surpassing eloquence, who attached to himself numerous followers, from admiration of his virtues and his power of speech, and that he so trained his friends and followers, that, though met together from different nations and endowed with diverse characteristics, they, nevertheless, lived sociably together in unity and concord, the gentle with the fierce, the quiet with the violent, the meek with the proud, the sensitive with the cruel. Then all of them gradually put off their ingrained faults, went after virtue and learned righteousness, exchanged shamelessness for a sense of shame, self-will for deference, ill-feeling for kindliness. But if ever anyone by his character had so much influence as to unite his friends and followers in mutual love for one another, you assuredly will accomplish this with far greater ease, for you were formed by nature before you were fitted by training for the exercise of all virtues. For before you were old enough to be trained, you were already perfect and complete in all noble accomplishments, before adolescence a good man, before manhood a practised speaker. But of all your virtues this even more than the others is worthy of admiration, that you unite all your friends in harmony. And I cannot conceal my opinion that this is a far harder task than to charm with the lyre the fierceness of lions and wild beasts: and you will achieve this the more easily, if you set yourself to uproot and utterly to stamp out this one vice of mutual envy and jealousy among your friends, that they may not, when you have shewn attention or done a favour to another, think that this is so much taken from or lost to themselves. Envy among men is a deadly evil and more fatal than any, a curse to enviers and envied alike. Banish it from your circle of friends, and you will keep them, as they now are, harmonious and kindly; but let it in any way spread among them, and it can only be stamped out with immense toil and immense trouble.

But prithee let us talk of better things. I love Julianus—for this discussion originated with him; I love all who are fond of you; I love the gods who watch over you; I love life for your sake; with you I love letters; like all your friends I take deep draughts of love for you.

Marcus Aurelius to Fronto

How would an emperor write a letter of praise to his former rhetorical teacher? Probably with every trick he could remember, if Marcus Aurelius' letter to Fronto is taken as an indication. Because praise and encomium were so important to rhetoric, expansive and polished letters of praise are typical of educated writers. In the following letter, Marcus praises Fronto for the friendship that Fronto had recently expressed in a letter. Note that Gratia is Fronto's wife.

Rome   143 c.e.
Transl. by C. R. Haines, *Correspondence of*
    M. C. Fronto, Ad M. Caes. 2.2 (LCL)

Marcus Aurelius to my most honourable consul, Fronto. I give in, you have won: beyond question you have conquered in loving all lovers that have ever lived. Take the wreath and let the herald, too, proclaim in the ears of all before your tribunal this your victory—"M. Cornelius Fronto, consul, is the winner. He is crowned in the contest of the Great Friendship-Games." Yet, though vanquished, will I not falter or fail in my devotion. Therefore shall you indeed, my master, love me more than any of men loves any man, while I, who have less energy in loving, will love you more than anyone else loves you, more, in fact, than you love yourself. I see I shall have a competitor in Gratia, and I fear that I may not be able to surpass her. For, as Plautus says, in her case, "not only has the rain of love drenched her dress with its thunder-drops, but soaked into her very marrow."

If you only knew what a letter you have written me! I could venture to say that she who bore me and nursed me, even she never wrote me anything so delightful, so honeyed. Nor is this due to your word-mastery or eloquence, for apply that test and not my mother only but all that breathe would, as they do, yield the palm at once to you. But I cannot express in words how that letter of yours to me, not for its eloquence or learning, but bubbling up as it does with so much kindness, brimful of such affection, sparkling with so much love, has lifted my heart up to the heavens, inspired it with the most glowing fondness, in a word, as Naevius says, filled it with a love transcendent.

Apollonius to the City Council of Caesarea

The bestowal of honor is most effective in a public setting. It is no surprise that letters of praise were inscribed in stone (e.g., Dittenberger, *OGIS* 223) and written to multiple recipients. There is scholarly debate about the authenticity of the letters attributed to the Neo-Pythagorean philosopher Apollonius of Tyana. At any rate, the letter to the city councillors of Caesarea illustrates how honor was bestowed and exchanged. For being honored by Caesarea, Apollonius returns a letter of praise. The writer uses two of the three terms characteristic of praising letters: to admire *(thaumazein),* to honor *(timan).*

Transl. by F. C. Conybeare, *Philostratus* 2,
   Letter 11 (LCL)

Men's first need is of gods for everything and above everything; their second of cities, for next after the gods we must honour our cities; and if we are men of sense we prefer our cities' welfare. Now if yours were only one city of many, instead of being, as it is, the greatest in Palestine, excelling all others there in size and in laws, and in institutions and in warlike virtues of ancestors, and still more in the arts and manners of peace, I should still see reason to admire and honour your city more than all others, and so would every man who has any sense. By common report this would be the reason for preferring your city on a comparison of it with the run of cities. But whenever a city leads the way in paying honour to a single individual, and that one who is a stranger, and comes from afar off, seeing that it is a city which honours him, what can the individual do by way of return, and what worthy repayment of yourselves is possible? This perhaps and none other: That if he is a man beloved of the gods by reason of some natural endowment, he should pray that that city may obtain all blessings, and that his prayer may be granted. This I shall never cease to do in your behalf, for I am pleased to see the manners of Hellenism revealing their own excellence, and doing it by means of public inscriptions. But as Apollonides the son of Aphrodisius is a young man of firm and constant character, and worthy to bear your name, I shall endeavour to render him of use to you in every particular, with the help of some good fortune.

Dorotheus to a Holy Man

Dorotheus forgot to add the recipient's name to the greeting in this letter. The recipient is almost certainly Paphnutius, however, since the letter was discovered together with six others addressed to him. Paphnutius was some kind of anchorite or holy man. Such figures were much revered by many in the fourth and fifth centuries, as the letter illustrates. Dorotheus' letter betrays literary skills which are a good deal above those usually found in the papyri. Like the writer of the papyrus letter to Sarapion (p. 28), Dorotheus does little beyond honoring the recipient.

Egypt   Fourth century C.E.
Transl. by H. I. Bell, *P.Jews* 1925

To the most valued brother and beloved of God. Dorotheus of Oxyrhynchus the unprofitable servant salutes you in the Spirit and in the love of Christ. Before all things I entreat God, the Father of our Saviour Jesus Christ, to vouchsafe that I may find favour in his sight, that you may receive my letter; for therein I too shall have cause to rejoice, when the good servant welcomes me in a letter and zealously offers up his prayers on my behalf to our Master in sincerity of heart. For I trust that . . . but by reason of your most glorious and most revered way of life, since you renounced the boasting of the world and abhorred the arrogance of the vainglorious. We too then commend you the more because we hear that you prudently showed forth your most noble contest, and we desire to imitate in the same way of life your kindliness (?), because God in abundant measure, it seems, granted you favour to find a fitting and salutary renunciation accordant with the times. For "redeeming the time," proclaims the thrice-blessed apostle, "because the days are evil." I trusted to behold your features also if the Lord permits it, since we are on the way, but I fear to come lest haply (you chide?) us and we be put to shame. We were very confident therefore that if it be God's will that we should meet you. You will first inform us by him that brings you the letter. Give him therefore the message whether you desire or not that we should come up, not so that . . . we fulfill . . . our love for you . . . concerning you, most valued in the Spirit, and the brethren who are with you.

Synesius to Heliodorus

The praising letters of Synesius, bishop of Cyrene, achieve the literary artistry to which the letter of Dorotheus only aspires. In the following letter to Heliodorus, Synesius praises a friend who according to Letter 17 had influence with the prefect of Egypt.

Cyrene   Late fourth or early fifth century C.E.
Transl. by Augustine Fitzgerald, *The*
   Letters of Synesius of Cyrene, Letter 17,
   p. 100

May all blessings fall to the lot of the man, whoever he is, inasmuch as he extols your dignity in pious reminiscences! He has filled the ears of all with your praises, those which are due to your heart of gold and to your tongue. However, you are promptly returning thanks for his good words. They are ever bringing him in return the praises of countless of your devoted friends, amongst whom I myself dispute the preeminence; nay, rather I dispute not at all, for all agree with me.

Letters of Blame *(memptikai)*

Blame *(psogos)* was the negative side of evaluative speech in antiquity. Rhetoricians did not divide blaming speech into subtypes, as they did praise (e.g., Menander Rhetor 331.15–24), but popular moral-philosophical rhetoric did. For our purposes the various types are best treated under types of exhortation (see pp. 125–141). Demetrius gives the following types which belong to the category of blame *(psogos)*: blaming *(memptikos)*, reproaching *(oneidistikos)*, censure *(epitimētikos)*, admonishing *(nouthetētikos)*, invective *(psek-tikos)*. Libanius treats five blaming types: blaming, reproaching, reproving *(elenktikos)*, maligning *(diablētikos)*. In addition, both handbooks treat the ironic letter, which was often considered to be blame in the form of mock praise. Obviously our English terms fail us here because our culture lacks these distinctions between types of blame. All of these types except invective and maligning can be types of exhortation. The letter of blame *(memptikē)* is the broadest and most basic of the letters that belong to the category of blame *(psogos)*.

Demetrius and Libanius are in agreement about the nature of the blaming *(memptikē)* letter. Demetrius writes:

> The blaming type is one that undertakes not to seem to be harsh. For example:

> Since time has not yet permitted you to return thanks for the favors you have received, (your failure to do so) is not the reason why I supposed it well not to mention what you have received. And yet you will (continue to) be annoyed with us, and impute words (to us). We do, then, blame you for having such a disposition, and we blame ourselves for not knowing that you are such a man.

Libanius says:

> The blaming kind is that in which we blame someone.

> The blaming letter. You did not act well when you wronged those who did good to you. For by insulting your benefactors, you provided an example of evil to others.

The letter of blame assumes an established positive relationship between writer and recipient. The writer is a benefactor of the recipient who feels that his favors have not received the right response. The recipient's behavior has not resulted in a display of the proper gratitude or reciprocity. The writer might be a king or wealthy patron of a certain city who writes to blame the citizens for an insult or a failure to honor him after receiving benefactions. But letters of blame occur on all social levels and in various social contexts. Perhaps the most commonly occurring situation is friends and family members blaming other friends or family members for failing to answer their letters. Blame is a response to a lack of reciprocity in a relationship. The blaming letter is, however, a mild form of censure since the writer wants to correct but maintain the positive relationship. The letter of blame, then, has the following fundamental elements:

1. The writer is the recipient's benefactor.
2. The recipient has wronged the benefactor.
3. The writer attempts to criticize and/or shame the recipient in such a way that he does not destroy their relationship.

The New Testament

Blame in the New Testament is best discussed under the various types of hortatory blaming letters. See pp. 125–141.

Horigenes to Serenus

Both papyrus and literarily transmitted letters that blame someone for failing to write are very common. The letter from Horigenes to Serenus is a typical papyrus example. The letter also includes an invitation. The theorists might have classified it as a mixed letter of invitation and blame. Many but by no means the majority of blaming letters use the expression "I blame you for . . ." (*memphomai*). Sometimes, like Paul in Galatians 1:6, the author uses the expression "I am surprised that . . ." (*thaumazō*) in order to express the complaint.

Oxyrhynchus, Egypt   Third century C.E.
P.Oxy. 2595
Transl. by author

Horigenes to Serenus his brother, greetings. I wish you to know that I make supplication for you every day to the gods of this place. You will do well to come to us for a few days. I blame you for not yet answering my letter. Salute the overseer and your brother Sarapammon and the governess and the whole household. (*2nd hand*) I pray for your health, brother. (*Verso*) Deliver to Serenus the silversmith.

Isias to Hephaistion

Hephaistion, the recipient of the letter from his wife Isias, is clearly in a bind. On the one hand, he has received a command from the god Sarapis to remain in the god's sanctuary at Memphis. On the other hand, his wife, who has anxiously awaited his return from the wars, believes that he is avoiding his duties and responsibilities to the family. Isias wrote this letter of blame, which was found at the Serapeum (temple of Sarapis). The meaning of the untranslated word *katochē* has been long debated by scholars. Whatever the exact meaning, it is a state that seems to have been commanded by a dream or vision of the god and included the obligation of staying within the temple precincts until released by the god. Isias begins on a positive note. This recalls *Papyrus Oxyrhynchus* 1837, where the writer criticizes the recipient's tactless use of blame: "No one who wants to make a charge or to blame someone writes it at the beginning of his letter lest the reader become offended and not read the letter."

Memphis, Egypt   168 B.C.E.
Transl. by Roger S. Bagnall, *Greek
Historical Documents*, 235

Isias to her brother Hephaistion (greeting). If you are well and other things are going right, it would accord with the prayer which I make continually to the gods. I myself and the child and all the household are in good health and think of you always. When I received your letter from Horos, in which you announce that you are in *katochē* in the Serapeum at Memphis, for the news that you are well I straightway thanked the gods, but about your not coming home, when all the others who had been secluded there have come, I am ill-pleased, because after having piloted myself and your child through such bad times and been driven to every extremity owing to the price of wheat, I thought that now at least, with you at home, I should enjoy some respite, whereas you have not even thought of coming home nor given any regard to our circumstances, remembering how I was in want of everything while you were still here, not to mention this long lapse of time and these critical days, during which you have sent us nothing. As, moreover, Horos who delivered the letter has brought news of your having been released from detention, I am thoroughly ill-pleased. Notwithstanding, as your mother also is annoyed, for her sake as well as for mine please return to the city, if nothing more pressing holds you back. You will do me a favor by taking care of your bodily health. Farewell. Year 2, Epeiph 30. *(Address)* To Hephaistion.

Lucius to Epagathus

Lucius Gemellus was the head of a household located in a village of the Fayum. Epagathus seems to have been his nephew and his household business manager. Gemellus blames Epagathus for driving pigs instead of transporting them by donkey cart and reminds him in a scolding way of instructions that he had previously given to him.

Fayum, Egypt   95–96 C.E.
Transl. by George Milligan, *Selections
from the Greek Papyri*, 66–67

Lucius Bellenus Gemellus to his own Epagathus, greeting. I blame you greatly for having lost two little pigs owing to the fatigue of the journey, seeing that you have in the village ten beasts able to work. Heraclidas the donkey-driver shifted the blame from himself, saying that you had told him to drive the little pigs on foot. I gave you strict charges to remain at Dionysias for two days until you had bought 20 artabas of lotus. They say that there is lotus to be had at Dionysias at the cost of 18 drachmas. As soon as you discover the price, by all means buy the 20 artabas of lotus, considering that it is essential. Hurry on the flooding of all the oliveyards . . . and water the row of trees in "the prophet." Do not fail in this. Goodbye.

Crates to Hipparchia

Crates was the famous Cynic follower of Diogenes. He was renowned for marrying Hipparchia who, naturally, also became a Cynic. In this fictitious Cynic letter (32), Crates blames Hipparchia for forgetting her Cynic training and lapsing back into the conventional life of a Greek woman. Notice how Crates softens the rebuke by approving of her concern for him. Letters of blame were, along with letters of admonition, the mildest forms of epistolary rebuke. They were to consist of constructive criticism that was not too harsh. Blame and admonition are sometimes difficult or impossible to distinguish, especially in philosophical letters.

Provenance unknown   First or second century C.E.
Text from Rudolph Hercher,
  Epistolographi Graeci
Transl. by author

Some people have come from you bringing a new tunic which they said you made so that I might have it for the winter. I approve *(apodechomai)* because you are concerned about me, but I blame *(memphomai)* you because you have not yet learned the appropriate behavior and are not living the philosophical life to which I exhorted you *(protrepō)*. Therefore, stop this behavior right now if you are truly concerned about me and do not pride yourself in this activity, but be serious about doing the things for which you wanted to marry me. Leave the wool spinning, which is of little value, to the other women who have aspired to none of the things to which you did.

Additional Examples

Praising Letters

For examples of praising letters see Plato, *Letter* 12; Apollonius of Tyana, *Letter* 12; Socratics, *Letter* 20; Pliny, *Letter* 4.18.

For Christian examples see *P.Jews* 1925, 1927; *P.Lond.* 3.1244, p. 244; *P.Oxy.* 1860; Cyprian, *Letter* 39; Basil, *Letters* 17, 50; Synesius, *Letters* 26, 49, 112; Augustine, *Letter* 58; Theodoret, *Letters* 60, 71.

Blaming Letters

For non-Christian examples see: *P.Oxy.* 1067, 1348; *Corp. Pap. Jud.* 2.444; *P.Par.* 47; *P.Merton* 112, 115; Plato, *Letter* 6; Apollonius of Tyana, *Letter* 46. For Christian examples see: Basil, *Letter* 12; Synesius, *Letters* 8, 23, 46, 138; and the hortatory letters of blame on pp. 125–141.

10

Letters of Exhortation and Advice

The terminology, types of literature, and traditions associated with exhortation and advice can be very confusing and require explanation. There is much overlapping and ambiguous terminology, which is partly due to the fact that exhortation was never systematically treated by the rhetoricians. Hortatory traditions (i.e., those concerning moral exhortation) played a part in popular moral pedagogy, philosophy, and rhetoric. *Paraenesis* is a Greek word frequently translated as "exhortation" but also as "advice." Other words such as *paraklēsis* and *protropē* are also translated as "exhortation." *Paraenesis* sometimes referred to content, that is, to traditional maxims or precepts of wisdom, especially moral wisdom. It could also refer to the form or process of moral teaching, that is, to the process of addressing words of encouragement or discouragement about behavior to a person or persons. Such moral teaching was originally poetic, as in Hesiod's exhortations to Perses (ca. 700 B.C.E.) and those of Theognis to Cyrnus (ca. 540 B.C.E.).

Isocrates and Aristotle in the fourth century B.C.E. provided the most important models for later hortatory literature and represent two poles in the use of moral exhortation. Isocrates' *To Nicocles* has many epistolary characteristics. It is advice addressed to a young king of Cyprus. By the use of examples and precepts Isocrates exhorts Nicocles to follow a certain model of the good ruler. Isocrates' model is very conventional and largely corresponds to traditional Athenian views of the good citizen and good leader. Aristotle's *Protrepticus* is also addressed to a ruler on the island of Cyprus. Although lost, the work has been substantially reconstructed from extensive fragments. Like a letter, the *Protrepticus* is actually addressed to Aristotle's royal friend rather than, as is often said, merely dedicated to him. The work may have been Aristotle's response to two of Isocrates' hortatory works, *Antidosis* and *To Nico-*

cles. It is certainly a competing and alternative kind of hortatory discourse, both in form and content.

While Isocrates' philosophy is life molded by traditional wisdom, Aristotle's is the new and radical life of contemplative and speculative wisdom from Plato's Academy. Aristotle urges Themison to give up the sorry goods of this world and to cultivate the intellectual aspect of the self which is in tune with the harmonies of the heavens and resembles God. Moral exhortation is always relative to some view of human flourishing. In Isocrates' vision, Nicocles is urged to keep on doing well what he has already begun to do and to conform to the highest expectations of the culture. Aristotle, on the other hand, calls Themison to a new kind of life in opposition to ordinary society. Isocrates' exhortation is confirmation literature, while Aristotle's is conversion literature.

The form of the *Protrepticus* corresponds to Aristotle's purposes. Although he employs some precepts and uses examples, an Isocratean assemblage of traditional examples and gnomic precepts would not do for Aristotle's unconventional purposes. Aristotle begins with propositions and argues, often syllogistically, to conclusions. Some member of Isocrates' school probably wrote the work *To Demonicus* as a response to the *Protrepticus*. The author of the former work criticizes those who write protreptic discourses to their friends urging a theoretical kind of philosophy which the author characterizes as mere skill in dialectic. Emphasis on argumentation as with Aristotle or on traditional wisdom formulated in traditional ways as with Isocrates would always remain poles of possibility within the hortatory tradition, although more characteristically the two approaches were mixed.

In this discussion I will use *protreptic* in reference to hortatory literature that calls the audience to a new and different way of life, and *paraenesis* for advice and exhortation to continue in a certain way of life. The terms, however, were used this way only sometimes and not consistently in antiquity. The distinction is always relative to the audience's disposition toward the new life. Paul's initial preaching activity by which he established the Thessalonian church may be considered protreptic discourse. In 1 Thessalonians he explicitly claims to be reminding them of teachings they received during his initial preaching activity. These teachings, however, are no longer protreptic but now paraenetic: 1 Thessalonians exhorts them to continue and grow in those things to which they were converted. This distinction is very useful but one should remember that Posidonius, Seneca, and others also used *paraenesis* or the Latin *praeceptio* for exhortation and moral-philosophical advice in general.

Thus paraenesis can mean either moral exhortation in general or moral exhortation that has a confirming and traditional character.

A question that has vexed both some theoreticians in antiquity and modern scholars is whether paraenesis should be distinguished from advice. If so, advice would concern specific, occasional matters (Shall we sail or go by land?)—and paraenesis would concern general, universal matters (The good man is honest). The fact is that paraenesis was not generally distinguished from advice and the terms *paraenesis* and *symboulē* (advice) were often used interchangeably. It is also true, however, that the distinction could be made, although practically it is very difficult to entirely separate traditional general advice from specific occasional advice. A closely related question is whether paraenesis or exhortation in general belongs to deliberative (i.e., advising) rhetoric or to epideictic rhetoric (the occasional rhetoric of praise and blame) (see p. 51). From one perspective Aristotle's *Protrepticus* can be considered an encomium in praise of contemplative philosophy and thus epideictic. From another view it can be seen as advice to Themison on how to live his life. Actually, both of these perspectives are correct. Exhortation transcends the rhetorical categories. This is not surprising since it was always on the fringes of that tradition and was only treated systematically by certain philosophers in conjunction with ethics.

By the time of the empire the authors of our sources generally recognize that there are several types of exhortation. Among types of exhortation (*monitio = paraenesis*), Seneca (*Letters* 94.39, 49; 95. 34, 65) mentions consolation (*consolatio*), warning (*dissuasio*), encouragement (*adhortatio*), censure (*objurgatio*), praise (*laudatio*), protreptic exhortation (*exhortatio*), and admonition (*admonitio*). Negative types of exhortation such as censure and admonition had always belonged to the tradition. In later times these negative types seem to have multiplied. The Christian writer Clement of Alexandria discusses eight types of hortatory blame in his *Instructor* (1.9). The epistolary handbooks also discuss several letters of blame and treat them as types of exhortation.

A useful distinction that I shall employ is between simple and complex hortatory letters. Words of exhortation were common to everyday language and can occur here and there in all types of letters. A letter may also, as a whole, follow the pattern of a certain type of exhortation, e.g., admonition. Many hortatory letters, however, mix various types of exhortation in characteristic ways. This is the case, for example, in the classic examples of paraenetic letters, which typically mix positive and negative types of simple exhortation in certain patterns. One particular mode of exhortation may predominate in a complex hortatory letter. What all complex letters of moral exhortation have in common is an explicit or implicit model of what it means to be a good person in general or a good person in a certain role. The rhetoric of exhortation, then, attempts to persuade and move the audience to conform to that model and to elicit corresponding habits of behavior. Authors also frequently use contrasting negative models.

Paraenetic Letters (Exhortation and Dissuasion)

Libanius' first type is a paraenetic letter. It is his longest discussion of a letter. He seeks to distinguish the paraenetic letter from the letter of advice. Demetrius gives a letter of advice but not a paraenetic letter. His model for the advising letter is very much like Libanius' paraenetic letter in contrast to the latter's insistence on distinguishing the two types. Libanius' discussion raises key issues about the definition of paraenetic letters, and his model suggests the essential elements of the type.

> The paraenetic style is that in which we exhort someone by urging him to pursue something or to avoid something. Paraenesis is divided into two parts, encouragement and dissuasion. Some also call it the advisory style, but do so incorrectly, for paraenesis differs from advice. For paraenesis is hortatory speech that does not admit of a counter-statement, for example, if someone should say that we must honor the divine. For nobody contradicts this exhortation were he not mad to begin with. But advice is advisory speech that does admit of a counter-statement, for example, if someone should say that we must wage war, for much can be gained by war. But someone else might counter that we should not wage war, for many things result from war, for example, defeat, captivity, wounds, and frequently the razing of a city.

> The paraenetic letter. Always be an emulator, dear friend, of virtuous men. For it is better to be well spoken of when imitating good men than to be reproached by all men while following evil men.

The paraenetic letter is not, as some have thought, a miscellaneous listing of commands. Libanius emphasizes that it involves both exhortation to something and dissuasion from something. In actual letters this positive and negative exhortation can occur in widely varying proportions and by different means. Sometimes the exhortation is antithetical: "Be like this but not like that." The author may also use distinct positive and negative sections. Contrasting virtues and vices and examples of character and behavior are also employed.

In his sample letter Libanius illustrates the essential characteristic of providing a positive model of behavior which the reader is either explicitly or implicitly urged to imitate. The model can be presented to the reader in various ways. A seemingly random series of precepts or virtues may actually provide an implicit pattern of character. Very frequently authors refer to historical and legendary examples. Sometimes letter writers also appeal to living examples, including examples of the author's own behavior that may be set forth for imitation.

Libanius' model letter also illustrates the typical friendly context of paraenetic correspondence. Paraenesis required some type of positive relationship, e.g., that of parent and child, or friendship. It was customary for the adviser to liken himself to a father exhorting his child. Friends were supposed to care for each other's character development. The author's self-presentation as a friend is often the relational framework for providing exhortation and specific advice.

The actual advice in Libanius' model letter is gnomic and unexceptional, as the author indicates paraenesis should be. The motivation for the advice is to be well spoken of and not reproached. Libanius believes that paraenesis concerns those basic and unquestioned patterns of behavior which are sanctioned by honor and shame. Thus he tries to distinguish paraenesis from advice. He thinks of advice along the lines of deliberative rhetoric: the rhetoric of the council where issues of expediency were debated. It is possible to find letters that are almost purely traditional advice and others that are almost purely specific and occasional. Many, however, mix the two (e.g., Cicero, *To His Brother Quintus* 1.1). Even when the material is almost purely traditional, the author has selected and edited it with a particular situation in mind. Demetrius' model letter of advice mixes characteristics that for Libanius would belong to both types.

Paraenesis in Libanius' sense was not supposed to teach anything that was essentially new. Writers either directed paraenesis at those who had already been initiated into a social group and needed to habituate the initial learning, or they considered the paraenetic exhortations to be universal and known to all. This does not mean that such known "teachings" could not be presented in creative ways or arguments given for why they ought to be followed. The basic elements in paraenesis are precepts, examples, discussions of traditional moral topics *(topoi),* encouraging reminders of what the readers already know and have accomplished, and reasons for recommended behavior. Paraenetic letters are generally dominated by encouraging types of exhortation, although words of admonition or mild rebuke here and there could be appropriate (e.g., Cicero, *To Friends* 5.14). Consolatory sections are also frequently parts of these complex letters of exhortation.

The paraenetic letter has the following fundamental elements:

1. The writer is the recipient's friend or moral superior (e.g., older, wiser, more accomplished).
2. The writer recommends habits of behavior and actions that conform to a certain model of character and attempts to turn the recipient away from contrasting negative models of character.

Complex paraenetic letters appear to have been written by those with a fair level of culture and education. I have not yet found any good examples among the papyri, although there are simpler exhortations in the papyri that suggest development toward more complex hortatory letters. The first examples below illustrate this phenomenon. Hortatory letters are most common among philosophers and highly educated writers of the upper classes. Fortune has preserved many such letters from Latin writers of the early empire. Christianity brought conscious moral pedagogy to its members on a scale heretofore unknown. Therefore, paraenetic and simple hortatory letters from Christians are to be found in great numbers.

The New Testament

Exhortation plays a major role in all the letters of Paul and the Pauline school except Philemon. This is also the case for Hebrews, James, 1 Peter, 1 and 2 John. First Thessalonians is an excellent example of a paraenetic letter (see bibliography on p. 178). First Corinthians is a complex paraenetic and advising letter. Paul's use of his own example and the example of Apollos is quite explicitly paraenetic rather than apologetic (1 Cor. 3:5–4:21; ch. 9). First Corinthians 4:14–21, for example, contains several features of paraenesis: "I admonish you" (14); Paul as father to the Corinthians, his children (15); "I exhort you" (16); the call to imitation (16); exhortation as reminding (17); antithesis (14, 15, 19, 20). First Corinthians also has characteristics of letters of advice in the narrower sense (see pp. 107–112), which, as I have emphasized, were quite frequently combined with traditional paraenesis.

The pastoral epistles compare well with fictitious paraenetic letters written in the names of philosophers. Second Timothy is a good example of a personal paraenetic letter. The portrait of Paul in these letters serves as a model that is commended to the purported recipients and indirectly to the intended real audience. The letters, then, present a model of following a model. First Peter is a complex hortatory letter which resembles those of Paul and the Pauline school in many ways. Hebrews is hortatory but, in general, does not resemble Greek and Latin hortatory letters because of its dominating exegetical argumentation. James consists of a series of seemingly disjointed hortatory *topoi* without any apparent unifying model or models.

Non-Christian paraenetic letters are usually addressed to individuals. In New Testament exhortation, the individual is not an object of guidance and character-building apart from the community. Paraenetic conventions, therefore, are adapted to community exhortation and plural address by the New Testament writers.

Esthladas to His Father and Mother

Esthladas' letter to his parents is an example of simple exhortation in a papyrus letter. The purpose of the letter is to provide encouragement for his mother and father. Here, unlike complex hortatory letters, there is no model of the good person or the good person in a certain role that either explicitly or implicitly informs his exhortations. In its fundamental structure, Esthladas' letter is just like Libanius' letter: In each case an exhortation to someone with whom the writer has a special positive relationship is followed by a reason for heeding the advice. Libanius' letter differs in putting forth the comprehensive model of the virtuous man rather than Esthladas' implicit conception of well-being for his parents.

Egypt   130 B.C.E.
Ed. Ulrich Wilcken, *Chrestomathie,* 10
Transl. by author

Esthladas to his father and mother, greetings and health. As I have often written you to be courageous and to take care of yourself until things have settled down, you would once again do well to exhort yourself and those who are with you to be courageous. For I have just discovered that Paos is sailing up

river in the month of Tubi with sufficient forces to subdue the
mobs at Hermonthis and to deal with them as rebels. Take care
of my sisters also and Pelops, Stachys and Senathuris. Farewell.
Year 40, Choiach 23. *(Address)* Deliver at Pathyris to my father.

Ammonius to Apollonius

Some believe the letter of Ammonius to be the earliest known
Christian papyrus letter. Although that is possible, there is nothing
in the letter to make it necessary. Ammonius and Apollonius may
have belonged to some kind of pagan religious or philosophical
group. Like many paraenetic letters, Ammonius' letter begins by
affirming the friendship between the correspondents and then
launches into advice giving. The exhortation is to peace and harmony among the "brothers." As in letters of advice and deliberative
rhetoric, Ammonius argues for what is useful or expedient in Apollonius' situation. A certain view of proper life together in some sort
of community or fellowship also seems implicit.

Oxyrhynchus, Egypt   Late first or early second century C.E.
Transl. by P. J. Parsons, *P.Oxy.* 3057

Ammonius to Apollonius his brother, greetings. I received
the crossed letter and the portmanteau and the cloaks and the
reeds, not good ones—the cloaks I received not as old ones, but
as better than new if that's possible, because of the spirit (in
which they were given). But I don't want you, brother, to load
me with these continual kindnesses, since I can't repay them—
the only thing we suppose ourselves to have offered you is (our)
friendship. Please *(parakalō)*, don't concern yourself further
with the key of the single room: I don't want you, my brothers,
to quarrel for my sake or for anyone else's; indeed I pray *(eu-
chomai)* for concord and mutual affection to maintain itself in
you, so that you can be beyond the reach of gossip and not be
like us: experience leads me to urge *(protrepsasthai)* you to live
at peace and not to give others a handle against you. So try and
do this for my sake too—a favour to me, which in the interim
you'll come to recognize as advantageous (to you as well). If
you've received the wool from Salvius to the full amount, and
if it's satisfactory, write back to me. I wrote you silly things in
my previous letter, which you'll discount: the fact is my spirit
relaxes when your name is there—and this though it has no
habit of tranquillity, because of its pressing troubles. Well,
Leonas bears up (?). My best wishes to you, master, and all your

people. Good health, most honoured friend. *(Address)* To Apollonius . . . , surveyor, his brother.

Aquila to Sarapion

In the following letter, Aquila encourages Sarapion, "the philosopher," in his pursuit of virtue through ascetic denial of worldly attractions. Aquila uses good paraenetic style when he congratulates Sarapion on what he has already attained and speaks of their pursuit of virtue as a common cause. Paul also begins his letters with encouraging compliments on the achievements of the congregations to which he is writing. As in Aquila's letter, this includes reports of testimony from others (e.g., Rom. 1:8; 1 Thess. 1:8–9). Aquila then sums up that which Sarapion is to avoid and to aspire to with a brief string of exhortations.

Oxyrhynchus, Egypt   Third or early fourth century c.e.
Transl. by P. J. Parsons, *P.Oxy.* 3069

Aquila to Sarapion, greetings. I was overjoyed to receive your letter. Our friend Callinicus was testifying to the utmost about the way of life you follow even under such conditions— especially in your not abandoning your austerities. Yes, we may deservedly congratulate ourselves, not because we do these things, but because we are not diverted from them by ourselves. Courage! carry through what remains like a man! Let not wealth distract you, nor beauty, nor anything else of the same kind: for there is no good in them, if virtue does not join her presence, no, they are vanishing and worthless. Under divine protection, I expect you in Antinoöpolis. Send Soteris the puppy, since she now spends her time by herself in the country. Good health to you and yours! Good health! *(Back)* To Sarapion the philosopher from his friend Aquila.

Seneca to Lucilius

The idea of guiding a protégé's character development over a period of time by means of letters goes back at least to Epicurus. The letters of Seneca to Lucilius, however, are the only extant extended correspondence of this sort from antiquity. Unfortunately, scholars who have continued to debate the "authenticity" of the letters have not made good use of the paraenetic letter tradition, and the question is still unresolved. Most of the letters follow patterns of relating precepts and reasons for precepts to models of behavior that are at least as old as Isocrates and his school. All of this is worked out within the personal framework of the friendly letter, whose commonplaces and conventions are made to serve paraenetic functions.

Like the apostle Paul and other writers of paraenetic letters, Seneca sometimes uses his own behavior as a model for imitation. This is the case in Letter 6, where Seneca's description of his own moral progress in the first part of the letter functions as a model for the pursuit of moral development to which he exhorts Lucilius in the second part. Paul does something similar in 1 Corinthians, Galatians, and 1 Thessalonians. As Seneca says (6.5), "The way is long if one follows precepts, but short and helpful if one follows examples."

Italy   Ca. 62–64 c.e.
Transl. by R. M. Gummere, *Seneca:*
  Epistulae Morales (LCL)

Seneca to his own Lucilius, greeting. I feel, my dear Lucilius, that I am being not only reformed, but transformed. I do not yet, however, assure myself, or indulge the hope, that there are no elements left in me which need to be changed. Of course there are many that should be made more compact, or made thinner, or be brought into greater prominence. And indeed this very fact is proof that my spirit is altered into something better—that it can see its own faults of which it was previously ignorant. In certain cases sick men are congratulated because they themselves have perceived that they are sick.

I therefore wish to impart to you this sudden change in myself; I should then begin to place a surer trust in our friendship —the true friendship, which hope and fear and self-interest cannot sever, the friendship in which and for the sake of which men meet death. I can show you many who have lacked, not a friend, but a friendship; this, however, cannot possibly happen when souls are drawn together by identical inclinations into an alliance of honourable desires. And why can it not happen? Because in such cases men know that they have all things in common, especially their troubles.

You cannot conceive what distinct progress I notice that each day brings to me. And when you say: "Give me also a share in these gifts which you have found so helpful," I reply that I am anxious to heap all these privileges upon you, and that I am glad to learn in order that I may teach. Nothing will ever please me, no matter how excellent or beneficial, if I must retain the knowledge of it to myself. And if wisdom were given me under the express condition that it must be kept hidden and not uttered, I should refuse it. No good thing is pleasant to possess, without friends to share it.

I shall therefore send to you the actual books; and in order that you may not waste time in searching here and there for profitable topics, I shall mark certain passages, so that you can turn at once to those which I approve and admire. Of course, however, the living voice and the intimacy of a common life will help you more than the written word. You must go to the scene of action, first, because men put more faith in their eyes than in their ears, and second, because the way is long if one follows precepts, but short and helpful, if one follows patterns. Cleanthes could not have been the express image of Zeno, if he had merely heard his lectures; he shared in his life, saw into his hidden purposes, and watched him to see whether he lived according to his own rules. Plato, Aristotle, and the whole throng of sages who were destined to go each his different way, derived more benefit from the character than from the words of Socrates. It was not the classroom of Epicurus, but living together under the same roof, that made great men of Metrodorus, Hermarchus, and Polyaenus. Therefore I summon you, not merely that you may derive benefits, but that you may confer benefit; for we can assist each other greatly.

Meanwhile, I owe you my little daily contribution; you shall be told what pleased me today in the writings of Hecato; it is these words: "What progress, you ask, have I made? I have begun to be a friend to myself." That was indeed a great benefit; such a person can never be alone. You may be sure that such a man is a friend to all mankind. Farewell.

Pliny to Avitus

Pliny also uses himself as an example for imitation in his letter to Avitus (2.6). He begins by recounting an incident where a dinner host displayed miserliness combined with self-indulgence. He then relates a conversation at the dinner where he took a stand against these vices by putting forth his own behavior as a contrast. Pliny thus employs the paraenetic device of antithetical models of behavior and then explicitly draws out principles of behavior. In the last section of the letter he exhorts Avitus to avoid excess and be temperate, explicitly citing the vices he is to avoid. In Letter 8.23.2 Pliny calls himself Avitus' moral guide and mentor. This letter well illustrates Pliny's moral guidance. One might compare Pliny's use of his dinner party confrontation to Paul's account of his confrontation with Peter in Galatians 2.

Italy   97–98 C.E.
Transl. by William Melmoth, revised by
   author

Pliny to his own Avitus, greeting. It would be a long story, and of no importance, were I to tell in too much detail how I happened to have dined recently with a man—though not his friend—who in his own opinion lives in splendid economy; but according to mine, in a sordid yet expensive manner. Some very elegant dishes were set before him and a few other guests; while those which were placed before the rest were cheap and mean. There were small flasks of three different sorts of wine; but not that the guests might take their choice, but rather, that they might not choose at all. One was for himself and me; the next for his friends of a lower rank (for, you must know, he measures out his friendship according to the degrees of quality); and the third for his own and our freedmen. One who sat next to me took notice of this, and asked me if I approved of it. "Not at all," I said. "What, then," he said, "do you do on such occasions?" "I give all my company the same fare; for when I make an invitation, it is to dine, not to classify my guests. Since they have all equally been invited to my table, I treat them as equals in everything." "Even the freedmen?" he asked. "Even them," I said; "for at my table they are not freedmen, but dinner companions." "That must cost you a great deal." I assured him not at all. "How could that be?" I said, "Because my freedmen don't drink the kind of wine I drink, but I drink what they do."

And certainly if a man is wise enough to moderate his own greed, he will not find it so very expensive to entertain all his visitors as he does himself. Restrain the greed for luxury and dress it down, if you want to be an economical host. You can do this better through moderation, than by insulting others.

The point of all this is to stop a young man of your excellent disposition from being tempted into the luxury which prevails at some men's tables, under the guise of frugality. And whenever I see any folly of this nature, I shall, because of the affection I bear you, point it out to you as an example which you ought to shun. Remember therefore, nothing is more to be avoided than this modern alliance of extravagance and meanness; qualities extremely odious when existing in distinct characters, but still more odious where they meet together in the same person. Farewell.

Pliny to Maximus

In his letter to Maximus (8.24), Pliny emphasizes the paraenetic commonplace that such advice is a reminder of what the addressee already knows and not new information (cf. 1 Thess. 1:5; 2:2, 5, 9, 11; 3:4, 6; 4:1, 9, 10; 5:1, 11). The selection of a paraenetic letter presupposes that the addressee is, in the writer's view, already substantially living and acting in the right way. Furthermore, the addressee already knows what is right and merely needs help in putting that knowledge into practice. The occasion for the advice is Maximus' recent assumption of the post of imperial legate in Achaia. The assumption of an office or the undertaking of a major task is a traditional occasion for paraenetic letters. Just this sort of situation is envisaged in the pastoral epistles (1 and 2 Timothy, Titus). Pliny's advice is traditional but adapted so as to address the particular occasion that is in view.

Italy   Ca. 100 C.E.
Transl. by B. Radice, *Pliny: Letters and Panegyricus* (LCL)

Pliny to his own Maximus, greeting. I know you need no telling, but my love for you prompts me to remind you to keep in mind and put into practice what you know already, or else it would be better for you to remain ignorant. Remember that you have been sent to the province of Achaia, to the pure and genuine Greece, where civilization and literature, and agriculture, too, are believed to have originated; and you have been sent to set in order the constitution of free cities, and are going to free men who are both men and free in the fullest sense, for they have maintained their natural rights by their courage, merits, and friendly relationships, and finally by treaty and sanction of religion. Respect the gods their founders and the names they bear, respect their ancient glory and their very age, which in man commands our veneration, in cities our reverence. Pay regard to their antiquity, their heroic deeds, and the legends of their past. Do not detract from anyone's dignity, independence, or even pride, but always bear in mind that this is the land which provided us with justice and gave us laws, not after conquering us but at our request; that it is Athens you go to and Sparta you rule, and to rob them of the name and shadow of freedom, which is all that now remains to them, would be an act of cruelty, ignorance and barbarism. (Illness is the same in a slave as in a free man, but you will have observed how a doctor will treat the free man with more kindness and consideration.) Remember what each city was once, but without looking down on it for being so no longer; do not allow yourself to be hard or domineering, and have no fear that you will be despised for this. No one who bears the insignia of supreme authority is despised unless his own meanness and ignobility show that he must be the first to despise himself. It is a poor thing if authority can only test its owners by insults to others, and if homage is to be won by terror; affection is far more effective than fear in gaining your ends. Fear disappears at your departure, affection remains, and, whereas fear engenders hatred, affection develops into genuine regard.

Never, never forget (I must repeat this) the official title you bear, and keep clearly in mind what it means to establish order in the constitution of free cities, for nothing can serve a city like ordered rule and nothing is so precious as freedom; nor can anything equal the disgrace should order be overthrown and freedom give place to servitude. You are moreover your own rival; you bring with you the excellent reputation you won during your quaestorship in Bithynia, you bring the Emperor's recognition and your experience as tribune, praetor, and holder of your present office, given you as a reward for your services. You must then make every effort not to let it appear that you were a better, kinder, and more experienced administrator in a remote province than in one nearer Rome, and when dealing with servile rather than free men, when you were elected by lot instead of being the Emperor's choice, and at a time when you were raw and unknown before being tested and proved by experience. And, besides, as you have often heard and read, it is far more shameful to lose a reputation than not to win one.

Please believe, as I said at the start, that this letter was intended not to tell, but to remind you of your duties—though I know I am really telling you as well, as I am not afraid of letting my affection carry me too far; there is no danger of excess where there ought to be no limits.

Augustine to a Christian Circle

Augustine was bishop of Hippo, a city of Roman Africa, in the early fifth century. He wrote Letter 210 to a group of individuals who were probably monastics. Augustine himself may have first brought monasticism to North Africa. This paraenetic letter employs various types of exhortation in complex ways. It contains warning, consolation, admonition, encouragement, and even advice about giving rebuke. The prescript, which names Augustine and the brethren with him as senders, echoes the Pauline prescript. Like Paul, Augustine also addresses a collective audience, although he also wrote paraenetic letters to individuals. Just as Seneca and other pagan writers use quotations in giving precepts, so Augustine also uses them but draws them from the scriptures rather than from the poets and philosophers.

North Africa   423 C.E.
Transl. by J. H. Baxter, *Saint Augustine:*
    Select Letters (LCL)

To the well-beloved and saintly mother Felicitas and brother Rusticus and the sisters who are with you, Augustine and the brethren who are with me send greeting in the Lord.

The Lord is good and everywhere His mercy is shed abroad, which comforts us with your love in Him. How greatly He loves those who believe and hope in Him and who love both Him and one another, and what blessings He stores up for them to enjoy hereafter, He shows most of all by this, that upon the unbelieving and the abandoned and the perverse, whom He threatens with eternal fire in company with the devil if they persist in their evil disposition unto the end, He nevertheless in this present world bestows so many benefits, making "His sun to rise on the evil and on the good and sending rain on the just and unjust." That is a brief sentence, meant to suggest further thoughts to the mind, for who can count up how many benefits and unearned gifts the wicked receive in this life from Him whom they despise? Among these is this great blessing, that by the instances of intermingled tribulation with which, like a good physician, He blends the charm of this world, He warns them, if they but pay heed, to "flee from the wrath to come" and to "agree, while they are in the way" (that is, in this life) with the word of God, which by their wicked lives they have made their "adversary." What, then, is not sent to men by the Lord God in His compassion, when even tribulation is a blessing sent by

Him? For prosperity is God's gift when He comforts us, while adversity is God's gift when He is warning us. And if, as I said, He furnishes these even to the wicked, what does He prepare for those who wait for Him? Among this number rejoice ye that by His grace you have been gathered, "forbearing one another in love, endeavouring to keep the unity of the Spirit in the bond of peace." For there will not fail to be occasion for your bearing with one another, until the Lord has borne you hence and "death is swallowed up in victory" and "God shall be all in all."

Yet in strife we ought never to take pleasure, though from time to time it is either born of love or puts love to the test. For who is easily found that is willing to endure reproof? And, what about that wise man of whom it is said, "Rebuke a wise man, and he will love thee"? Surely then we ought not to refrain from reproving and correcting a brother in case he go down to death in false security. It is a usual experience and a common occurrence for one who is reproved to be mortified at the time and to wrangle and be recalcitrant, yet afterwards to reflect within himself in silence, alone with God, where he is not afraid of displeasing men by being reproved, but is afraid to displease God by refusing correction, and thenceforward to refrain from doing the thing for which he was justly rebuked, and in proportion as he hates his sin, to love the brother whom he realizes to have been the enemy of his sin. But if he belongs to the number of those of whom it is written, "Rebuke a fool and he will go on to hate thee," the contention is not born of his love, but yet it tries and tests the love of his reprover, since he does not repay hatred with hatred, but the love which prompted his rebuke endures undisturbed, even when he who was rebuked requites it with hatred. If the reprover, however, choose to render evil for evil to the man who takes offence at being reproved, he was not fit to reprove another, but clearly fit to be reproved himself. Act upon these principles, so that occasions of provocation may either not arise among you, or, when they do occur, be immediately quenched in speedy peace. Strive more earnestly to disseminate harmony among yourselves than to encourage faultfinding, for just as vinegar corrodes a vessel if it remain too long in it, so anger corrodes the heart if it linger on to another day. "These things, therefore, do, and the God of peace shall be with you." At the same time pray for us, that we may with cheerful mind carry out the good advice we have given you.

Letters of Advice *(symbouleutikai)*

Although it is very often difficult to distinguish letters of exhortation from letters of advice *(symbouleutikai)*, it can be done and there are nonhortatory letters of advice. As we have seen, Libanius criticizes those who do not make that distinction. Demetrius' example of a letter of advice reveals some of the difficulties of maintaining Libanius' distinctions.

> It is the advisory type when, by offering our own judgment, we exhort (someone to) something or dissuade (him) from something. For example, in the following manner:

> I have briefly indicated to you those things for which I am held in high esteem by my subjects. I know, therefore, that you, too, by this course of action can gain the goodwill of your obedient subjects. Yet, while you cannot make many friends, you can be fair and humane to all. For if you are such a person, you will have a good reputation and a secure office among the masses.

In general, it is difficult to fit the literature of the hortatory tradition completely into either epideictic or deliberative, i.e. advising, rhetoric. When advice calls for a specific course of action it is deliberative; when it only seeks to increase adherence to a value or to cultivate a character trait it is epideictic. Exhortation typically transcends these categories and shares characteristics of both. But when Libanius criticizes the identification of paraenesis with advice, he is thinking of advice strictly in terms of deliberative rhetoric. Demetrius' summary description of the advisory letter is in agreement with Libanius on this point. He says that the writer exhorts or dissuades from something by offering his own judgment. In advising a course of action the author does not merely commend traditional precepts or wisdom, but advances his own opinion. Deliberative was usually defined as the rhetoric of public debate where the speaker advanced arguments from expediency in order to exhort someone or dissuade someone from a future course of action. Demetrius applies this to the more private situation of the letter of advice.

When Demetrius gives his sample letter, however, it more closely resembles Libanius' paraenetic letter than the letter of advice modeled solely on a strict definition of deliberative rhetoric. In it, one ruler gives advice to another ruler. In a paraenetic manner, he uses himself as an example to provide exhortation on how to rule well. There is no specific and occasional question of expediency. Instead, the exhortations are clearly based on a model of the good ruler. The advisor's own judgment is only a factor to the extent that he claims his own experience to be a confirmation of the model. The actual advice about the ruler's relationship to subjects and friends is in fact based on traditional clichés.

Advice in the stricter deliberative sense is specific and occasional. A specific request for advice concerning a matter often provides the stimulus for a letter of advice. Sometimes an advising letter answers a series of questions from an inquiring letter. Advising should not be confused with commanding. Even when older or socially higher advisors speak strongly and with authority, they still give reasons and seek to persuade. Taking advice is not a matter of obedience. Arguments from expediency are central to deliberative rhetoric, although other arguments, e.g., the just, the good, the natural, often play a supporting role. Letters of advice, above all, contain arguments that move from past experience and precedent to what is advantageous or disadvantageous. In very rare instances, letters of advice are even clearly arranged according to the parts of deliberative speeches: proem, proposition, proof, epilogue. One such letter is Cicero's *To Friends* 110, where he attempts to persuade Cato to vote for his triumph.

The letter of advice in the strict deliberative sense contains the following fundamental features:

1. The writer is older, wiser, or more experienced than the recipient.
2. The writer tries to persuade or dissuade the recipient with regard to some particular course of action in the future.

The New Testament

Paul very skillfully mixes exhortation and specific advice in 1 Corinthians. Chapters 1–4 are structured around the paraenetic use of Apollos' and Paul's own examples, which lead to admonition and examples of the Corinthians' own lack of judgment, i.e., 5:1–13 and 6:1–11. Although the latter texts are admonitory, they are also advising since Paul recommends specific actions. In 6:12–20 he introduces the deliberative argument from expediency, which is recapitulated and amplified in 10:23–11:1 in connection with a paraenetic call for imitation. Paul develops himself as a model for imitation not only in chapters 1–4 but also in chapter 9. Chapters 7–8 and 10–14 provide advice that is recommended by many different kinds of argumentation. These, however, center on expediency in achieving a high quality of community in the time before the return of Christ. Chapters 13 and 15 amplify advice into exhortation.

Second Corinthians is even more complex. It seems to mix exhortation, advice, rebuke, invective, and apology. Chapters 8 and 9 are clearly a kind of advice and exhortation. Much of the remainder of 2 Corinthians can be seen as Paul's attempt to dissuade the Corinthians from choosing to follow other teachers and to recognize Paul as their spiritual father. Apology and advice thus work together in Paul's argumentation.

Exhortation and advice are also skillfully mixed in Galatians. The narrative in 1:13–2:21 presents Paul as a model of one who has died to the law, a Jew who has taken up the life through Christ offered to Gentiles apart from the law. Paul's larger argument seeks to dissuade the Galatians from receiving circumcision and exhorts the Gentile Galatians to the community of the Spirit apart from the law. Thus Paul both seeks to dissuade them from a future action (advice) and exhorts them to continue in the life they have already begun (paraenesis).

The Letters of Chairemon and Sarapion

The two following papyrus letters illustrate a typical problem the investigator encounters in studying papyrus letters of advice. It is sometimes difficult to distinguish advising letters from commanding letters. There are two reasons for this. First, advice is often given with little or no supporting argumentation in the papyri: The writer depends on a positive personal relationship more than on argumentative persuasion. Second, the social relationship between recipient and writer is often unclear. Chairemon is probably a friend or relative although not an actual brother of Eudaimon in the following letter. The imperatives are meant as advice that he is urging Eudaimon to follow and that he hopes will seem reasonable. In Sarapion's letter, it is not clear whether Heraclides is a slave, business agent, client, or friend. Therefore, it is unclear whether Sarapion is giving commands or advice. Unlike the case of commanding letters, giving reasons or the assumption of reasonableness is essential to the letter of advice. Its basic premise is that the recipient has the freedom finally to decide for himself or herself. The conditional—"If this, then this; otherwise . . ." and "Do this but"—is typical of much argumentation in letters of advice. One might profitably compare such Pauline texts as 1 Corinthians 7 and 8.

Egypt   Third or fourth century C.E.
Transl. by G. H. R. Horsley, *NDIEC*
(1981), p. 60

Chairemon to Eudaimon his brother, greetings. You will act rightly, brother, to exhibit as perfect your kindness and your goal. If our sister is alone do all you can to send her with your mother. Otherwise, let her be in your hands. And write back to me with regard to what is fitting. And try hard to send her to Alexandria. But if you see that she is in difficulty and cannot come, write back to me. . . . Exhibit as perfect your kindness. . . . I greet you and your wife and all yours. Send the copies to me quickly to your father's. *(2nd hand)* I pray you are well. *(Verso)* [. . .] from Chairemon [. . .]

Egypt   41 C.E.
P.Oxy. 299
Transl. by author

Sarapion to our Heraclides, greeting. I sent two other letters to you, one by Nedymus and one by Cronius the sword-bearer. Subsequently, I received your letter from the Arab and I read it with distress. Offer your services to Ptollarion at all times; perhaps he can help you. Say to him, "I am different, different from all the rest. I am a child [*or* slave (?)]. I have sold you my merchandise for a talent too little [*or* except for a talent's worth (?)]. I do not know what my patron will do to me. We have many creditors. Do not ruin us." Beg him every day. Perhaps he will pity you. If not, like everyone else, you also ought to beware of the Jews. By offering your services to him, you stand a better chance of gaining his friendship. See if you can get the tablet signed by Diodorus' help through the wife of the prefect. If you see to your own business, you can't be blamed. Salute Diodorus heartily. Farewell. Year One of Tiberius Claudius, Caesar Augustus Germanicus Imperator, the eleventh of the month Caesareus. *(Address)* Deliver in Alexandria in the Imperial Market in [. . .] to Heraclides from Sarapion.

Speusippus to Xenocrates

In this fictitious letter, Speusippus advises Xenocrates to return to Athens and assume the leadership of Plato's Academy. Speusippus urges that this is the right thing for Xenocrates to do, arguing from Xenocrates' respect for and gratitude toward Plato. Papyrus letters tend to offer various "bits" of advice; literarily transmitted letters of advice often argue for one point in detail.

Provenance unknown   Ca. 200 C.E.
Transl. by David Worley, in *The Cynic*
  Epistles (ed. Malherbe), p. 297

I considered it my duty not to overlook any of the things that are good, both because of Plato's command and because of the friendship which exists between you and me. I thought I should write you about my physical condition, and also because I think that if you come to the Academy you will keep the School together. I shall try to show you that this is right and proper. Plato, as you also know, held the School in the Academy in no ordinary esteem, thinking it to be something which leads to the right kind of reputation, and which contributed to his own life and to the later preservation of his memory among men. This being so, he confirmed at his death that he held you in high regard. He enjoined all of us who belong to his household, if something should happen to you, to bury you next to him, for he thought that you would not at all separate yourself from the Academy. It therefore appears to me especially fitting that you should honor both the living and the dead Plato, for it becomes an accomplished gentleman to pay careful attention to his gods, ancestors, and benefactors. One would find that Plato's asso—ciation with his friends agrees most closely with what has been said. He cared for some as a father, for others as a bene-factor; and in general in the opinion of everyone he held the place of a god. Considering it to be good and proper, I advise you to show the greatest gratitude to Plato, and to do so especially in a way appropriate to him. You would do so by returning to the Academy and keeping the School together. One might fairly call reliability and faithfulness true wisdom. We should in these things be very different from the majority of men. But you appear to be more diligent than duty requires.

Pliny to Geminus

In Letter 7.1 Pliny gives Rosianus Geminus medical advice based on his own experience and opinions. Pliny explicitly connects his advice with his own example and, in a way common to the hortatory tradition, presents his advice as a project that advisor and advisee have in common.

Italy   107 C.E.
Transl. by W. Melmoth, revised by
     author

Pliny to his own Geminus, greeting. This obstinate distemper
which hangs upon you greatly alarms me; and though I know
how extremely temperate you are, yet I am afraid your disease
should get the better of your character. Let me advise you then
to bear it with patient endurance; this is sound advice and the
course to recovery. There is nothing impossible in what I recommend. It is a rule which, at least while in good health, I make
a practice of giving my household: "I hope, that should I be
attacked with any disorder, I shall desire nothing of which I
either ought to be ashamed, or have reason to be sorry; however, if my distemper should prevail over my resolution, I for-
bid that anything should be given me but by the consent of my
physicians; I warn you that if you do, I shall punish your compli-
ance, as much as another man would your refusal."

I had once a most violent fever; when the fit was a little
abated, and I had been anointed, my physician offered me
something to drink; I held out my hand and asked him to check
my pulse, and instantly returned the cup, though it was just at
my lips. Afterwards, when I was preparing to go into the bath,
twenty days from the first attack of my illness, perceiving the
physicians whispering together, I inquired what they were saying. They replied, they were of the opinion I might possibly
bathe with safety; however, they were not without some suspicion of hazard. "Why," I said, "should I do it at all?" And thus
I quietly gave up the pleasure I was on the point of enjoying,
and abstained from the bath with the same composure I was
going to enter it. I mention this, not only in order to enforce
my advice by example, but also that this letter may be a sort of
pledge upon me to persevere in the same resolute abstinence
for the future. Farewell.

Protreptic Letters (Exhortation to a Way of Life)

No theorist or rhetorician ever defined the protreptic letter in
antiquity. It was neither a recognized type nor a widely used kind
of letter. Nevertheless, it is important for those who have an interest
in early Christian letter writing. Protreptic in this semitechnical
sense means those writings which fall broadly into the tradition of

protreptikoi logoi (protreptic speeches), of which Aristotle's *Protrepticus* and Cicero's *Hortensius* are the most famous examples. These are exhortations to take up the philosophical life. Protreptic speeches can be traced back to the Sophists, who tried thereby to win students to their schools and to the wisdom which they taught. Protreptic works urge the reader to convert to a way of life, join a school, or accept a set of teachings as normative for the reader's life. A *protrepticus* may combine two or even all three of these goals.

Although there were protreptic exhortations to various arts (e.g., Galen's protreptic to medicine), the genre is dominated by philosophy. Protreptic writings were important to Christianity because of its strong missionary impulse. Christian protreptic speech ranges from missionary sermons to major philosophical-theological works like Clement of Alexandria's *Protrepticus*. Most Christian and non-Christian protreptic letters are, as one would expect, on the shorter and less formal side. They are often friendly letters with a few encouragements and brief argumentation that serves as an invitation for the reader to take up the way of life in question. Both Christians and pagans also wrote longer protreptic letters that not only exhort their audience to the life which they advocate, but also introduce them to their teachings and beliefs in a more comprehensive way. Some so-called apologies like the *Epistle to Diognetus* and Tatian's *Oration Against the Greeks* are actually protreptic works.

The approach that writers took to their protreptic tasks varied according to their views of human nature and the human situation. Most protreptic works not only attempt to exhort their audience to something but also seek to turn them away from something. One approach is to refute objections against the particular kind of philosophy or Christianity in question and to argue for its advantages or superiority. If the author believes that the uninitiated must overcome a serious moral-character problem before they can be opened to the new life, then, admonition, censure, or rebuke might play a central role in the protreptic work. Epictetus argues that genuine philosophical protreptic does not use the flattering invitation of epideictic rhetoric (*Discourses* 3.23). Instead, genuine protreptic must make the hearer realize his evil plight, cast aside self-conceit, come to himself, and recognize his need for a teacher. This equation of the protreptic process with the achievement of self-knowledge goes back at least to the protreptic speech of Socrates in Plato's *Euthydemus*.

The New Testament

In both form and function, Paul's letter to the Romans is a protreptic letter. Paul introduces the Romans to his gospel and at the same time also presents himself as a master teacher. It thus serves as an introduction and invitation to the teaching activity Paul hopes to do at Rome. Paul explains his gospel of salvation for the Gentiles and argues that Jewish failure to accept that gospel will not mean a loss of Israel's salvation. Throughout chapters 3–11 Paul answers objections to this gospel made by an imaginary Jewish discussion partner. Also in a protreptic manner, he censures the attitudes of arrogance and pretentiousness that prevent Jews and Gentiles from accepting his gospel to the Gentiles (see Rom. 2:1–6, 17–24; 3:1–9; 3:27–4:2; 9:19–21; 11:13–32; 14:4, 10).

Epicurus to His Mother

The Epicureans manifested a kind of missionary impulse, although its similarity to the Christian mission has been exaggerated. Starting in 1884, French and Austrian archaeologists discovered parts of a wall that had been inscribed with several Epicurean texts by a certain Diogenes of the Lycian city of Oenoanda. Diogenes of Oenoanda lived in the second century C.E., leaving this public proclamation of the Epicurean philosophy "out of compassion" for his fellowmen. Among the discoveries from the wall were fragments of a letter from Epicurus to his mother.

Epicurus' mother had apparently written to him saying that she had seen him in a dream. It is not clear whether the dream somehow frightened her or merely produced anxiety about his safety. At any rate, Epicurus used the opportunity to urge his mother to join him in the philosophical life. He begins by saying that there is no real difference between the perception of those absent and those present, a point from Epicurean perception theory. Epicurus gave dreams and memory of loved ones a positive role in his philosophy: They served as a substitute for the actual presence of friends. He then urges his mother not to worry since he is making great progress in the attainment of happiness. In this way, Epicurus becomes a protreptic model for her. After this, he probably went on to argue that not only dreams of absent loved ones but even death cannot destroy happiness. (The text at this point is fragmentary.) The dead feel nothing and loved ones always have happy memories of them. Epicurus, then, encourages her not to worry about his needs.

In what is probably the final part of the letter, Epicurus explicitly urges his mother to give up the speeches of rhetoricians and to listen instead to the gospel of his own philosophy. The letter is protreptic both because of Epicurus' attempt to persuade his mother of fundamental doctrines, i.e., in arguing for the superiority of beliefs and practices that constitute the particular way of life, and also in being an invitation for her to become a student of those teachings.

The arrangement I have made of the fragments is probably the correct order, but complete certainty is not possible, since parts of the letter are missing.

Provenance unknown   Ca. 311 B.C.E.
Texts and transl. of Frags. 52–53 from
    C. W. Chilton, *Diogenes of Oenoanda*,
    pp. 19–20; and of Frags. 3 and 24,
    respectively, from M. F. Smith, *AJA*
    74(1970): 61, and *AJPh* 99(1978): 331

[. . .] (to cause the greatest concern about them. For the appearance of those who are absent, independent of sight, instills very great fear, whereas if they are present with us it causes not the least dread. But if you carefully examine their nature the appearances) of the absent are exactly the same as those of the present. For being not tangible but intelligible they have in themselves the same capacity towards those present as when they arose, their subjects being present also. Therefore, Mother, take heart; you must not regard visions of me as evil. Rather consider that I am daily acquiring useful help towards advancing further towards happiness. Not slight or of no avail are the advantages that accrue to me, such that they make my condition equal to the divine and show that not even mortality can make me inferior to the indestructible and blessed nature. For as long as I live I rejoice even as do the gods [. . .].

These people are not easily helped, even when they are afraid of death. [. . .] the same, if he suffers diminution; but if he has no sensation, how is he diminished? Surrounded by such good things, then, think of me, Mother, as rejoicing always and have confidence in how I am faring. But in heaven's name be sparing with the remittances you are constantly sending me. I do not wish you to be in need so that I may have abundance, I would rather suffer need so that you should not; and yet I am living in plenty in every respect thanks to friends and father continually sending me money; indeed only recently Cleon sent me nine minae. So neither one nor other of you should worry about me but enjoy each other's company [. . .].

(For at present you reject our philosophy but later perhaps you will wish, when your hostility has been banished,) to open the calm entrances to our community, and you will turn away from the speeches of the rhetoricians in order that you may hear something of our tenets. After that we confidently hope that you too very quickly will knock at the doors of philosophy.

Epicurus to Menoeceus

Unlike the one to his mother, Epicurus' letter to Menoeceus is complete. It is also too long to present here in its entirety. It is much more essay-like and less occasional than the protreptic letter to his mother. Perhaps the letter was Epicurus' intentional counter to Aristotle's *Protrepticus*. The letter urges Menoeceus to take up the study of philosophy and exhorts him to follow Epicurus' ethical teachings, which are briefly summarized. As often in protreptic works, after introductory exhortations Epicurus first argues against false views. In this case he counters false views of the gods and death, which produce unhappiness. In the next section of the letter, Epicurus summarizes and recommends his philosophy of the good life. He discusses pleasure as a standard of the good, the practical calculus of pursuing pleasure, and finally, the centrality of prudence as a means to pleasure.

Athens or Asia Minor   Third century B.C.E.
Transl. by Cyril Bailey, *Epicurus*, 83–93

Let no one when young delay to study philosophy, nor when he is old grow weary of his study. For no one can come too early or too late to secure the health of his soul. And the man who says that the age for philosophy has either not yet come or has gone by is like the man who says that the age for happiness is not yet come to him, or has passed away. Wherefore both when young and old a man must study philosophy, that as he grows old he may be young in blessings through the grateful recollection of what has been, and that in youth he may be old as well, since he will know no fear of what is to come. We must then meditate on the things that make our happiness, seeing that when that is with us we have all, but when it is absent we do all to win it.

The things which I used unceasingly to commend to you,

these do and practice, considering them to be the first principles of the good life. First of all believe that god is a being immortal and blessed, even as the common idea of a god is engraved on men's minds, and do not assign to him anything alien to his immortality or ill-suited to his blessedness: but believe about him everything that can uphold his blessedness and immortality. For gods there are, since the knowledge of them is by clear vision. But they are not such as the many believe them to be: for indeed they do not consistently represent them as they believe them to be. And the impious man is not he who denies the gods of the many, but he who attaches to the gods the beliefs of the many. For the statements of the many about the gods are not conceptions derived from sensation, but false suppositions, according to which the greatest misfortunes befall the wicked and the greatest blessings (the good) by the gift of the gods. For men being accustomed always to their own virtues welcome those like themselves, but regard all that is not of their nature as alien.

Become accustomed to the belief that death is nothing to us. For all good and evil consists in sensation, but death is deprivation of sensation. And therefore a right understanding that death is nothing to us makes the mortality of life enjoyable, not because it adds to it an infinite span of time, but because it takes away the craving for immortality. For there is nothing terrible in life for the man who has truly comprehended that there is nothing terrible in not living. So that the man speaks but idly who says that he fears death not because it will be painful when it comes, but because it is painful in anticipation. For that which gives no trouble when it comes, is but an empty pain in anticipation. So death, the most terrifying of ills, is nothing to us, since so long as we exist, death is not with us; but when death comes, then we do not exist. It does not then concern either the living or the dead, since for the former it is not, and the latter are no more.

But the many at one moment shun death as the greatest of evils, at another (yearn for it) as a respite from the (evils) in life. (But the wise man neither seeks to escape life) nor fears the cessation of life, for neither does life offend him nor does the absence of life seem to be any evil. And just as with food he does not seek simply the larger share and nothing else, but rather the most pleasant, so he seeks to enjoy not the longest period of time, but the most pleasant. . . .

When, therefore, we maintain that pleasure is the end, we do not mean the pleasures of profligates and those that consist in sensuality, as is supposed by some who are either ignorant or disagree with us or do not understand, but freedom from pain in the body and from trouble in the mind. For it is not continuous drinkings and revellings, nor the satisfaction of lusts, nor the enjoyment of fish and other luxuries of the wealthy table, which produce a pleasant life, but sober reasoning, searching out the motives for all choice and avoidance, and banishing mere opinions, to which are due the greatest disturbance of the spirit.

Of all this the beginning and the greatest good is prudence. Wherefore prudence is a more precious thing even than philosophy: for from prudence are sprung all the other virtues, and it teaches us that it is not possible to live pleasantly without living prudently and honourably and justly, (nor, again, to live a life of prudence, honour, and justice) without living pleasantly. For the virtues are by nature bound up with the pleasant life, and the pleasant life is inseparable from them.

For indeed who, think you, is a better man than he who holds reverent opinions concerning the gods, and is at all times free from fear of death, and has reasoned out the end ordained by nature? He understands that the limit of good things is easy to fulfill and easy to attain, whereas the course of ills is either short in time or slight in pain: he laughs at (destiny), whom some have introduced as the mistress of all things. . . .

Meditate therefore on these things and things akin to them night and day by yourself, and with a companion like to yourself, and never shall you be disturbed waking or asleep, but you shall live like a god among men. For a man who lives among immortal blessings is not like to a mortal being.

Anacharsis to Croesus

Anacharsis was a Scythian prince who visited Greece in the sixth century B.C.E. As the legend developed, he became the noble barbarian. In the Cynic letters of Anacharsis he represents the simple natural life and serves as a critic of the luxury and artificiality of Greek culture. The letter is protreptic because Anacharsis urges Croesus to renounce luxury and vice and to take up the natural life of virtue. The "discourse on kingship," a genre favored by philosophers, was closely related to the protreptic discourse. Aristotle and Isocrates both addressed their protreptic works to rulers. The idea behind this practice was that if you converted the ruler, the subjects would follow. This also helps to explain the protreptic nature of many so-called Christian apologies to emperors. A protreptic letter to a king, then, even a fictitious one like Anacharsis' Letter 9, represents a well-known and significant kind of literature.

The admonishing-rebuking element is very strong in this letter. The author begins this censure with a story of civilization's decline that might profitably be compared to chapter 1 of Paul's letter to the Romans. Anacharsis then accuses Croesus of falling into the same sort of vice and urges him to renounce his unnatural life of luxury. The hortatory section is followed by a parable of robbers and a grounded ship. In the final part of the letter, he puts forward the Scythians as models of the natural life and urges Croesus to consider how he will live out his life.

Provenance unknown   Third century B.C.E.
Transl. by Anne M. McGuire, in *The
    Cynic Epistles* (ed. Malherbe), pp.
    47–51

The Greek poets in their poetry distributed the universe among the sons of Chronos, and assigned to one the sphere of heaven, to the second that of the sea, and to the third that of the nether darkness. This distribution arose from the Greeks' pursuit of their own interests. For as they know nothing of mutual participation in anything, they ascribe their own evil to the gods. The earth, however, even they excepted and left it the common possession of all.

Come, let us consider the consequences of this thought. They wished all the gods to be honored by men, and all of them to be dispensers of good and averters of evil. The earth was long ago the common possession of the gods and of men. In time, however, men transgressed by dedicating to the gods as their private precincts what was the common possession of all. In return for these, the gods bestowed upon men fitting gifts: strife, desire for pleasure, and meanness of spirit. From a mixture and a separation of these grew all the evils which afflict all mortals: tilling the soil, sowing, metals, and wars. For although they sowed very liberally, they harvested but little, and although they worked at various crafts, they found only a short-lived luxuriousness. They sought the treasures of the earth in various ways, and deemed their search a wonderful thing! They regard as most blessed the first man who devised this silly little undertaking. They do not know that like children they deceive themselves. For first they prized nothing that comes by toil, and then they admire toil itself.

I have heard that this evil which befalls most men has befallen you, too. From this evil, others follow. For neither great wealth nor possession of fields has ever bought wisdom. For, it is said, those persons whose bodies are filled with many foreign things will also be filled with diseases. And they urge those who desire to be healthy to escape as quickly as possible. Because of your immoderate enjoyment of pleasure you have physicians for your bodies, but not for your souls. It would be wise for you to renounce pleasure. When much gold flows toward you, the fame that attaches to gold and the envy and desire of those who wish to rob you of your gold have flowed toward you, too, together with the gold. If, therefore, you had purified yourself of the disease, you would have become healthy, speaking and ruling freely. For this is what it means for a king to be healthy. If you had this inward possession, it would be no wonder if you also acquired the virtues. But the disease, laying hold of you in your incontinence, plunged you into ruin, and made you a slave instead of a free man. But be of good courage and consider the image of a fire which originates in a forest and turns what catches on fire to ashes, but which is fed by what is unburnt. So the evils which were yours long ago have passed over to those who have a hold on you and your possessions. Expect that the sorrows will come to those after you, and hear a story which I myself witnessed.

Through the land of the Scythians there flows a great river, which is called the Danube. On this river, some merchants ran their ship aground on a reef. Since they could not budge it in any way, they went away lamenting. So, when robbers, without understanding the problems of these men, sailed up with an empty ship, they freely loaded cargo, and at once transferred the cargo from the strange ship, unaware of the calamity as they made the transfer. For as the one ship was emptied, it started to float and become seaworthy. But the ship taking on the other's cargo quickly sank to the bottom because of the robbery of foreign goods.

This can always happen to the person who has possessions. But the Scythians have stood apart from all of these things. All of us possess the whole earth. What it freely gives, we accept. What it hides, we dismiss from our minds. We protect our cattle against wild beasts, and in return receive milk and cheese. We have weapons, not to attack other people, but to defend ourselves, if it should be necessary. And it has not as yet been necessary. For we are set before those who would attack us as combatants and as prizes of combat at the same time. For not many men welcome this prize of combat kindly. These same things Solon, the Athenian, also advised you, urging you to consider the end. He was not speaking of what transpires in the present, but he was saying that you should prefer that by means of which you will finish your life well. He did not say this openly, for he was not a Scythian. But as for you, if it pleases you, take my advice to Cyrus and to all tyrants. For it will flourish better among those in power than among those who are ruined.

Crates to Aper

In Letter 35, Crates calls on Aper to adopt the Cynic life. After introductory reasoning followed by the conclusion that conventional social life cannot lead to happiness, the writer presents contrasting possibilities for life. There is the way of softness which is folly, and hardship which is wisdom. The author concludes by putting forward two antithetical models for imitation—the masses or Socrates and Diogenes.

Provenance unknown   First or second century C.E.
Transl. by Ronald F. Hock in *The Cynic*
    Epistles (ed. Malherbe), p. 89

To Aper, do well. The oracle of the ancients, honored Sir, has given advice that is concise and fitting in regard to every circumstance: Do not flee from what is necessary. For the one who flees from what is inevitable must be unhappy, and the one who desires what is impossible must fail to obtain it. Perhaps, then, I shall seem to you to be rather importunate and pedantic, and I do not defend myself against this charge. And yet, if it does seem so to you, condemn me, but pay attention to the ancients. For I have concluded from my own case that we men are distressed precisely when we wish to live a life without hardship. But this wish is impossible. For we must live with the body, and we must live with men as well, and most hardships issue from the folly of those who live in society, and in turn, from the body. If, therefore, a wise man lives by these principles, he is free from pain and confusion, a happy man. But if he is ignorant of these principles, he will never cease from being dependent on vain hopes and from being constrained by desires. As for you, then, if you are satisfied with the life of the masses, make use of those advisors, for in fact they are more expert in these matters. But if the life of Socrates and Diogenes pleases you, leave the writings of the tragic poets to others and devote yourself to emulating those men.

The Letter to Diognetus

The author of this Christian protreptic letter is unknown and its date of composition uncertain. It has often been classed as an apology but its real purpose was missionary not defensive. In a way typical of protreptic works, the author begins with the negative side of his case: Pagan religion and Judaism, the alternatives to Christianity, are first criticized. The author then presents a positive picture of the Christian life-style and expounds Christian beliefs. The hortatory element is always present and the letter concludes with a tactful and somewhat indirect call for Diognetus to become a Christian. The following excerpts provide a good sense of the writer's approach.

Provenance unknown   Second or third century C.E.
Transl. by Kirsopp Lake, *The Apostolic
    Fathers* (LCL)

Since I perceive, most excellent Diognetus, that you are exceedingly zealous to learn the religion of the Christians and are asking very clear and careful questions concerning them, both who is the God in whom they believe, and how they worship him, so that all disregard the world and despise death, and do not reckon as God those who are considered to be so by the Greeks, nor keep the superstition of the Jews, and what is the love which they have for one another, and why this new race or practice has come to life at this time, and not formerly; I indeed welcome this zeal in you, and I ask from God who bestows on us the power both of speaking and of hearing, that it may be granted to me so to speak that you may benefit so much as possible by your hearing, and to you so to hear that I may not be made sorry for my speech.

Come then, clear yourself of all the prejudice which occupies your mind, and throw aside the custom which deceives you, and become as it were a new man from the beginning, as one, as you yourself also admitted, who is about to listen to a new story. Look, not only with your eyes, but also with your intelligence, what substance or form they chance to have whom you call gods and regard as such. Is not one a stone, like that on which we walk, another bronze, no better than the vessels which have been forged for our use, another wood already rotten, another silver, needing a man to guard it against theft, another iron, eaten by rust, another earthenware, not a whit more comely than that which is supplied for the most ordinary service? Are not all these of perishable material? Were they not forged by iron and fire? Did not the wood-carver make one, the brass-founder another, the silversmith another, the potter another? . . .

In the next place I think that you are especially anxious to hear why the Christians do not worship in the same way as the Jews. . . .

For the distinction between Christians and other men, is neither in country nor language nor customs. For they do not dwell in cities in some place of their own, nor do they use any strange variety of dialect, nor practice an extraordinary kind of life. This teaching of theirs has not been discovered by the intellect or thought of busy men, nor are they the advocates of any human doctrine as some men are. Yet while living in Greek and barbarian cities, according as each obtained his lot, and following the local customs, both in clothing and food and in the rest of life, they show forth the wonderful and confessedly strange character of the constitution of their own citizenship. They dwell in their own fatherlands, but as if sojourners in them; they share all things as citizens, and suffer all things as strangers. Every foreign country is their fatherland, and every fatherland is a foreign country. They marry as all men, and they bear children, but they do not expose their offspring. They offer free hospitality, but guard their purity. Their lot is cast "in the flesh," but they do not live "after the flesh." They pass their time upon the earth, but they have their citizenship in heaven. They obey the appointed laws, and they surpass the laws in their own lives. They love all men and are persecuted by all men. They are unknown and they are condemned. They are put to death and they gain life. "They are poor and make many rich"; they lack all things and have all things in abundance. They are dishonoured, and are glorified in their dishonour, they are spoken evil of and are justified. "They are abused and give blessing," they are insulted and render honour. When they do good they are buffeted as evil-doers, when they are buffeted they rejoice as men

who receive life. They are warred upon by the Jews as fo-
reigners and are persecuted by the Greeks, and those who
hate them cannot state the cause of their enmity. . . .

Having thus planned everything by himself with his Child he
suffered us up to the former time to be borne along by unruly
impulses as we willed, carried away by pleasures and lust. Not
at all because he delighted in our sins, but in forbearance; not
in approval of the time of iniquity which was then, but fashion-
ing the time of righteousness which is now [. . .], he did not hate
us nor reject us nor remember us for evil, but was long-suffering, endured us, himself in pity took our sin, himself gave his
own Son as ransom for us, the Holy for the wicked, the innocent
for the guilty, the just for the unjust, the incorruptible for the
corruptible, the immortal for the mortal. For what else could
cover our sins but his righteousness? In whom was it possible
for us, in our wickedness and impiety, to be made just, except
in the Son of God alone? O the sweet exchange, O the inscruta-
ble creation, O the unexpected benefits, that the wickedness of
man should be concealed in the one righteous, and the righteousness of the one should make righteous many wicked! Having convinced us then of the inability of our nature to attain life
in time past, and now having shown the Saviour who is able to
save, even where it was impossible, it was his will for both
reasons that we should believe on his goodness, and regard him
as nurse, father, teacher, counsellor, physician, mind, light,
honour, glory, strength, life, and to have no care for clothing
and food.

If you also desire this faith, and receive first complete knowledge of the Father [. . .] For God loved mankind for whose sake
he made the world, to whom he subjected all things which are
in the earth, to whom he gave reason, to whom he gave mind,
on whom he enjoined that they should look upward to him,
whom he made in his own image, to whom he sent his only-
begotten Son, to whom he promised the kingdom in heaven—
and he will give it to them who loved him. And when you have
this full knowledge, with that joy do you think that you will be
filled, or how greatly will you love him who thus first loved you?
But by your love you will imitate the example of his goodness.
And do not wonder that it is possible for man to be the imitator
of God; it is possible when he will. For happiness consists not
in domination over neighbors, nor in wishing to have more
than the weak, nor in wealth, and power to compel those who
are poorer, nor can anyone be an imitator of God in doing these

things, but these things are outside his majesty. But whoever takes up the burden of his neighbour, and wishes to help another, who is worse off in that in which he is the stronger, and by ministering to those in need the things which he has received and holds from God becomes a god to those who receive them —this man is an imitator of God. Then, though your lot be placed on earth you will see that God lives in heaven. . . . Then you will marvel at those who endure for the sake of righteousness the fire which is for a season, and you will count them blessed when you know that other fire.

Letters of Admonition *(nouthetētikai)*

In popular culture there were widely shared agreements about the character and usage of various types of hortatory blame. Philosophers and philosophical traditions accepted, modified, or rejected the popular beliefs and practices about blame, depending on their views of the human condition and the methods considered necessary for a cure. Plutarch recommended the use of a very carefully nuanced and gentle admonition. Crates, one of the milder sort of Cynics, might have agreed. The harsher ascetic type would have insisted that only the amputation and cautery of reproaching *(oneidizein)* and reviling *(loidorein)* could save the vice-ridden masses. Dio Chrysostom, who often spoke to the masses, tended toward a harsher line but also saw the need for gentleness and for adapting his speech to individual needs. The student of hortatory blame must begin by realizing that authors and groups evaluated types of hortatory blame differently in spite of broad agreement on certain points. It is often difficult for the modern student to distinguish types of blaming letters. This is partly because the lines between the types were drawn at different places by different individuals and groups in antiquity. Writers, however, had no difficulty in communicating distinctions between types of hortatory blame when they considered the distinctions to be significant.

The most gentle type of blame was admonition *(nouthetein)*. Demetrius includes the admonishing type of letter *(nouthetētikē)* in his handbook:

The admonishing type is one which indicates through its name what its character is. For admonition *(nouthetein)* is the instilling of sense *(nous)* in the person who is being admonished, and teaching him what should and should not be done. In the following manner:

You acted badly when you ill-treated a man who had con-
ducted himself well and had lived according to reason, and who
had, generally speaking, done you no harm. Realize, therefore,
that this action deserves an apology. Indeed, if *you* had suffered
at the hands of someone else, you would certainly be justified
in expecting an apology from him. Do not, then, think that the
person who would rebuke sins had neither parents nor (proper)
upbringing, nor, worst of all, that he has no relative or friend.

Predictably, Demetrius begins with the common cliché about the
word's components: *nouthetein* means to instill understanding *(nous)*.
Clement of Alexandria *(Instructor* 1.9.76) defines it as "the censure
characterized by loving care which produces understanding *(nous)."*
Writers frequently said that admonition produces *sōphrosynē,* which
"literally" means "sound understanding" but is usually translated
by such words as temperance, self-control, moderation, modesty,
and sober-mindedness. Furthermore, the moralist used admonition
in order to bring about *metanoia,* i.e., repentance, a change of mind
(e.g., Plutarch *How to Tell a Flatterer from a Friend* 68F). In contrast
to the oft-repeated nonsense that pagan *metanoia* only produced
intellectual change whereas Jewish and Christian *metanoia* produced
"deeper transformations," moralists claimed that admonition
caused shame and deeply affected ethical dispositions (e.g., Plutarch, *On Moral Virtue* 452c). Plutarch says that well-delivered and
well-received admonition ought to reform the character, penetrate
like a biting drug, humble the hearer, produce dizziness and sweat-
ing, and burn the soul with shame *(On Listening to Lectures* 46D).
Socrates successfully admonished Alcibiades so that "he drew an
honest tear from his eyes . . . and turned his heart" *(How to Tell a
Flatterer* 69F).
      Demetrius also follows tradition in associating admonition with
teaching *(didaskein).* They were not synonymous but often linked
and admonition was said to have a didactic component. For Demetrius this teaching consists of moral precepts and advice which ac-
company the exposure and criticism of wrong.
      Widely voiced agreements existed concerning the characteristics
of good admonition. Blame that was truly hortatory was said to be
beneficial to the hearer (Isocrates, *Panegyric* 130; Seneca, *Letters*
44.36; 99.32; Dio Chrysostom, *Oration* 33.10–11; Plutarch, *How to
Tell a Flatterer* 66E). Admonition was gentle and its goal was to
reclaim a person from moral error as, for instance, in the gnomic
saying: "Admonition differs greatly from reproach *(oneidizein).* For
the former is both gentle and loving, while the latter is harsh and

violent. Admonition corrects people's sins but reproach only censures" (*Gnomologion Byzantinum* 59, p. 176; Wachsmuth). The motive of the admonisher is essential. Criticism that is motivated by anger, self-regard, or self-interest is merely blame *(mempsis)* and not admonition (Plutarch, *How to Tell a Flatterer* 66E).

Plutarch discusses strategies by which the exhorter can soften his admonition and make it more effective (*How to Tell a Flatterer* 70–72). One tactic is to mix praise with the blame in admonition. Another is to include oneself in the criticism by speaking in the plural, e.g., "we should not" or "people should not." The moralist should be very cautious about admonishing a person in public or before people respected by the recipient of the criticism. Public criticism can cause severe shame. Once when Pythagoras publicly admonished a disciple, the man was so shamed that he killed himself. Thereafter Pythagoras never admonished anyone except in private. Plutarch advises the use of indirect admonition when possible and tells the following story.

> But some persons manage more cleverly, and by finding fault with strangers, turn their own intimate acquaintances to repentance; for they accuse the others of what they know their own acquaintances are doing. My professor, Ammonius, at an afternoon lecture perceived that some of his students had eaten a luncheon that was anything but frugal, and so he ordered his freedman to chastise his own servant, remarking by way of explanation that "that boy can't lunch without his wine!" At the same time he glanced towards us, so that the rebuke took hold of the guilty. (*How to Tell a Flatterer* 70E)

The letter of admonition has the following basic elements:

1. The writer is the recipient's friend, peer, or moral superior (e.g., older, wiser, more accomplished).
2. The writer attempts to expose and constructively criticize certain aspects of the recipient's behavior so that the latter can understand and amend the behavior.

The New Testament

Admonition is used very consciously and explicitly in the letters of Paul and the Pauline school. Members of the communities are also urged to practice admonition (e.g., Col. 3:16; 1 Thess. 5:12–14) and Colossians describes the Pauline mission to the Gentiles as teaching and admonition that leads to maturity in Christ (1:28).

Romans is a protreptic letter that makes central use of indirect admonition by means of censorious address to imaginary interlocutors in the style of the diatribe (2:1–5, 17–29; 9:19–20; 11:13–25; 14:4, 10). Paul acknowledges the admonitory character of the letter in 15:14–15: "I am confident . . . that you are able to admonish one another. But in some parts (of the letter) I have written to you very boldly in order to remind you." This is a rather typical (see, e.g., the letter from Sempronius below) assertion of the audience's lack of need for admonition which reflects the kinship between paraenesis and admonition. Admonition is correction for those whose moral health is fundamentally good. It is encouragement which reminds them to live up to what they are. Paul's call for "amendment" in 12:1–3 and his metaphor of reforming the understanding (e.g., 12:2–3; cf. 8:5–8) are also in the style of admonition.

First Corinthians mixes admonition with paraenesis and advice. Admonition plays an important role in the paraenesis of 1:10–4:20. Paul admonishes the Corinthians because of strife and exhorts them to unity. He is quite explicit in 4:14: "I am not writing these things to shame you, but to admonish you as my beloved children." "Shaming" was associated with harsher forms of blame (see pp. 133–141 below). Also see 1 Corinthians 5–6; 11:2–34 (admonition softened with praise); and 14:6–39. Like Philo, Clement of Alexandria, and others, Paul believes that scriptural narratives provide evaluative typologies of behavior that are to function as exhortation and admonition in the Christian communities (10:11).

Second Thessalonians 3:6–12 admonishes certain people in the community and 3:15 urges members to admonish one another. Somewhat as in Romans, James also employs diatribal address for indirect admonition (e.g., 4:13–5:6).

Sempronius to Maximus

This very simple letter of admonition was appended to another letter addressed to Saturnila, the mother. Sempronius addressed the packet to Maximus probably knowing that since his mother could not read, only Maximus would see the admonishing letter. Sempronius accuses his brother of treating their mother harshly, calls for him to change his behavior, and provides reasons through an appeal to traditional sayings about honor toward parents. Much like Paul in Romans 15:14–15, Sempronius tells Maximus to take the admonition in the right spirit and to realize that it reflects a basic confidence in him.

Egypt   Second century C.E.
*SB*3, 6263, 18–31
Transl. by author

Sempronius to Maximus his brother, many greetings. Before all I pray for your welfare. I learned that you are treating our revered mother harshly. Please, sweetest brother, do not cause her grief in any way. If any of the brothers talk back to her, you ought to hit them. For now you should be called father. I know that you are able to please her without me writing this letter, but do not take my letter of admonition in the wrong way. For we ought to worship her who bore us as a god, especially since she is good. I have written these things to you, brother, knowing the sweetness of our revered parents. Please write to me about your welfare. Farewell, brother.

Crates to Lysis

In fictitious Letter 10, Crates the Cynic admonishes Lysis for drunkenness. Crates' gentle, positive criticism is combined with paraenesis that urges Lysis to be temperate.

Provenance unknown   First or second century C.E.
Transl. by Ronald F. Hock, in *The Cynic
Epistles* (ed. Malherbe), pp. 61–63

Crates to Lysis. I have heard, Lysis, that you have constantly been drunk ever since the contest in Eretria. If this is true, it behooves you not to despise what the wise Homer says. For he says, "Wine destroyed even a centaur, the renowned Eurytion" [*Odyssey* 21.295], and also Cyclops, even though he possessed superhuman size and strength. Therefore, if wine adversely affects those who are stronger and greater than we are, how do you think it will affect us? Wretchedly, I think. In order, then, that nothing unpleasant happen because of it, I advise you to learn to put it to good use. So, it is absurd to think that one should not succumb to the plectrum, which does not drive those who use it well out of their minds nor throw them into madness, but to think that one should succumb to wine and use it. (Or does something so much worse result from the plectrum? Also be careful in using it.) Now, try to learn to use it temperately, and in the company of temperate men, so that the gift of God might not come down on your head because you dishonor it, but so that, because you do honor it, the pleasures that come from it might be enjoyed without regret and might be beneficial to you, especially when everyone causes you to live decently and justly, with temperance in the pleasures that are being limited, as you do nothing indecent or bad in your life, but say and do everything that is just. By their presence men are said to become thrice-blessed as three benefits accrue to them in life. For how would those men not be blessed who have temperate souls, healthy bodies, and sufficient possessions? In order, therefore, that you may enjoy these benefits, I exhort you not to slight these precepts.

Pliny to Tiro

Pliny's letter to Tiro (*Letter* 9.5) is a model of gentleness and indirectness in giving admonition. Pliny begins with praise and assures Tiro that he is not really guilty of the error which the letter criticizes. Nevertheless, Pliny says that he feels it necessary to add warning to his praise.

Italy   107–108 c.e.
Transl. by William Melmoth, revised by
    author

Pliny to his own Tiro, greeting. You are to be applauded for the mildness with which, as I am informed (and I make very strict enquiry), you administer justice in your province; one principal branch of which is to distinguish merit in every degree, and so to gain the love of the lower rank, as to preserve at the same time the regard of their superiors. But it is an error many have fallen into, that while they endeavour to avoid the appearance of favouring the great, they run into the contrary extreme, and gain the character of acting with ill manners, or ill nature. A mistake this, which you are far from committing, I well know: however, I cannot resist throwing in a caution with my applause, and recommending that you conduct yourself in such a manner as to keep up the distinctions of rank and dignity. For to level and confound the different orders of mankind, is far from producing an equality among them; it is, in truth, the most unequal thing imaginable. Farewell.

Pliny to Terentius Junior

Like the previous letter, this one (9.12) illustrates how the mildest forms of admonition are akin to paraenesis. In this case Pliny finds no specific fault in Terentius but offers advice in the form of an admonitory warning. The only criticism is the one implied in assuming that the recipient is in need of such a specific warning. As in paraenesis, Pliny also bases the exhortation on a personal example.

Italy   106–108 C.E.
Transl. by William Melmoth, revised by
  author

Pliny to his own Junior, greeting. A certain friend of mine lately corrected his son with great severity before me, for spending too much money on dogs and horses. And I said to him (when the youth had withdrawn), "Didn't you ever do anything yourself which deserved your father's correction? In fact, are you not sometimes even now guilty of errors which your son, were he in your place might reprove with equal severity? Are not all mankind subject to such mistakes? Have we not each of us our particular foibles in which we fondly indulge ourselves?"

The great affection I have for you has induced me to set this instance of unreasonable severity before you, as a caution not to treat your son with too much rigor and austerity. Consider that he is but a boy, and that there was a time when you were also. Therefore, in exerting the authority of a father, remember always that you are a man, and the parent of a man. Farewell.

Basil to Ubricius

Admonition could have a strong didactic component. Philosophers often held that improper conduct was due to false beliefs. Basil praises the monk Ubricius and then admonishes him and the Christian community with which he was associated for false beliefs. The teachings which Basil criticizes are associated with Apollinaris. The bishop concludes Letter 262 with a call for correction.

Caesarea   377 C.E.
Transl. by R. J. Deferrari, *Saint Basil: The
  Letters* (LCL)

You have done well in writing to us, for you have exhibited the fruit of charity in no small degree; and do you continue to do this. Do not, however, think that you need apologize whenever you write to us. For we understand ourselves and realize that to every man belongs by nature equality of like honour with all men, and that superiorities in us are not according to family, nor according to excess of wealth, nor according to the body's constitution, but according to the superiority of our fear of God. Therefore what is there to prevent you, who fear the Master more, from being greater than us on this very ground? So write to us continually, and inform us how the brethren about you are, and who of your church are sound, that we may know to whom we should write and in whom we may rest content. But since I hear that there are some falsifying the correct teaching about the incarnation of the Lord by distorted assumptions, I urge them through your Charity to refrain from that absurd view which some are reported to us as holding— that God Himself was turned into flesh, and did not assume through the Holy Mary the stuff from which Adam was moulded, but that He Himself through His own divinity was transformed into the material nature.

But this absurd opinion is very easy to refute. Yet since the blasphemy is manifest at a glance, I think that for one who fears the Lord even the mere reminder is enough. But far be it from me either to say this or to think it, since God has said: "I am, and I change not." Besides, how did the benefit of the incarnation pass to us, unless our body, united with the divinity, became superior to the domination of death? For if He had been turned, He could not have kept the substance of His own body, and just that still subsisted when His divine nature had become gross. And how could the divinity that is without bounds have been circumscribed within the bulk of a small body, even if it were true that the entire nature of the Only-begotten was "turned"?

But I believe that no one who has sense and possesses the fear of God suffers from this weakness. But since the report came to me that some of those who live with your Charity are within the grasp of this mental weakness, I thought that our letter ought not merely to carry a bare greeting, but ought to contain some such matter as might also strengthen the souls of those who fear the Lord. Accordingly we urge this—that you obtain ecclesiastical correction and abstain from communion with heretics, realizing that indifference in these matters takes away our liberty in Christ.

Letters of Rebuke *(epitimētikai)*

Rebuke was generally considered to be harsher than admonition. While some thought that admonition ought to cause at least mild shame, shame was essential to rebuke. Rebuke was directed at fundamental flaws of character or a basic pattern of "immoral" behavior. The rebuker tried to shame the sinner into stopping the misbehavior and often explicitly called for a change to an honorable way of life. Clement of Alexandria defines rebuke precisely: "Rebuke is blame because of what is shameful, reconciling (the person) to what is noble" (*Instructor* 1.9.77). Demetrius and Libanius are in agreement about the nature of the rebuking *(epitimētikē)* letter. Demetrius writes:

> The rebuking type is that written with rebukes on account of errors that have already been made. In the following manner:
>
> Some sins are committed voluntarily and some involuntarily, some are major and some minor, some are harmful only to those who commit them, while others are harmful to other people as well. But, your sins were like a way of life with you, for indeed you did not unwillingly commit sins that are great and harmful to many. It is therefore fitting that you meet with a more severe rebuke, if indeed in the present case it has happened that others also have been wronged. Nevertheless, the trespass that has occurred can still find healing. For if you aim at correction in your behavior, you yourself will cause it not to happen (again) as it had happened before.[10]

Shaming also occurs in Libanius together with an exhortation to stop sinning. Libanius' model letter does not contain a positive call to a new pattern of behavior.

> The rebuking genre is that in which we rebuke someone for what he has done indecently.
>
> The letter of rebuke. Well then, be ashamed for what you have done wrong, stop sinning, and do not live your life as an exercise in error. For, on account of you, we are disgraced.

Cicero cautions that rebuke *(objurgatio = epitimēsis)* is sometimes necessary but that like cautery and amputation it should only be used when milder forms of blame have failed (*On Duties* 1.38.136). Plutarch says that hortatory blame produces repentance and shame: Repentance is a kind of pain *(lypē)* and shame a kind of fear *(phobos)*. Both shame and repentance were strongly associated with rebuke.

Nevertheless, many writers urged that like admonition, rebuke was most effective when it was not too harsh and the positive purposes of the rebuker were clear. The emperor Julian holds up Crates the Cynic as a model for rebuke: "He would reconcile his closest friends when he learned they had quarrelled, and he rebuked them without being harsh but with charm and not so as to seem to be harming those whom he wanted to reform but as though he wished to benefit both them and others who were present" (*Oration* 6.201c).

The New Testament

Paul uses rebuke in his letter to the Galatians (e.g., 1:6–10; 3:1–5; 4:8–10). His expression "I am amazed" (1:6) and his denunciation of them as "fools" (3:1, 3) are characteristic of rebuke. He does, however, seek to soften his censure by reminding them of their relationship in Christ (4:12–20). In 2 Corinthians (7:8–10; cf. 2:1–7), Paul uses terminology for rebuke in speaking about a letter he had sent to the Corinthians: "so that even if I caused you pain *(lypē)* with my letter, I am not sorry (though I was sorry). . . . I rejoice, not that you were grieved *(elypēthēte),* but because you were grieved into repenting *(eis metanoian)."* Some at Corinth had apparently complained that Paul's letters of hortatory blame were too harsh (2 Cor. 10:1–12).

Apollonius to Ptolemaeus

Ptolemaeus was a devout believer in divine revelations through dreams. The temple of Sarapis, where Ptolemaeus was a devotee, was a favorite place for people who sought such revelations. Ptolemaeus, who is Apollonius' elder brother, had apparently convinced Apollonius to take some action based on a dream. The whole affair turned out badly and now Apollonius writes to shame his brother and warn him of the dire consequences of their trust in dreams. Apollonius' shaming rebuke might have been even harsher were it not for the fact that he too was involved in the shame.

Memphis, Egypt   Ca. 152 B.C.E.
Transl. by A. S. Hunt and C. C. Edgar,
    Select Papyri (LCL), p. 289

Apollonius to Ptolemaeus his father, greeting. I swear by Sarapis but for the fact that I am somewhat ashamed, you would never have seen my face again; for you utter nothing but lies and your gods likewise, for they have plunged us into a deep mire in which we may die, and when you have a vision that we are to be rescued, then we sink outright. Know that the runaway will try to prevent us remaining in the place; for because of us he has suffered a loss of 15 talents. The strategus is coming up tomorrow to the Serapeum and will spend two days in the Anubieum drinking. Never again can I hold up my head in Tricomia for shame that we have given ourselves away and been deluded, misled by the gods and trusting in dreams. Farewell. *(Address)* To Ptolemaeus, greeting. *(Added at the side)* A reply to the soothsayers.

Seneca to Lucilius and to Marullus

Seneca's Letter 99 is an instructive example of how types could be creatively mixed. It is a letter of consolation in the form of a rebuke for excessive grief. Instead of the customarily soothing consolation, Seneca turns traditional consolatory topics into rebukes. The following excerpts come from the beginning and ending of the rather lengthy letter.

Italy   Ca. 62–64 C.E.
Transl. by R. M. Gummere, *Seneca:*
   Epistulae Morales (LCL)

Seneca to his own Lucilius, greeting. I enclose a copy of the letter which I wrote to Marullus at the time when he had lost his little son and was reported to be rather womanish in his grief—a letter in which I have not observed the usual form of condolence: for I did not believe that he should be handled gently, since in my opinion he deserved criticism rather than consolation. When a man is stricken and is finding it most difficult to endure a grievous wound, one must humour him for a while; let him satisfy his grief or at any rate work off the first shock; but those who have assumed an indulgence in grief should be rebuked forthwith, and should learn that there are certain follies even in tears.

Is it solace that you look for? Let me give you a scolding instead! You are like a woman in the way you take your son's death; what would you do if you had lost an intimate friend? A son, a little child of unknown promise, is dead; a fragment of time has been lost. We hunt out excuses for grief; we would even utter unfair complaints about Fortune, as if Fortune would never give us just reason for complaining! But I had really thought that you possessed spirit enough to deal with concrete troubles, to say nothing of the shadowy troubles over which men make moan through force of habit. Had you lost a friend (which is the greatest blow of all), you would have had to endeavour rather to rejoice because you had possessed him than to mourn because you had lost him.

But many men fail to count up how manifold their gains have been, how great their rejoicings. Grief like yours has this among other evils: it is not only useless, but thankless. Has it then all been for nothing that you have had such a friend? . . .

Let us say this also to him who mourns and misses the untimely dead: that all of us, whether young or old, live, in comparison with eternity, on the same level as regards our shortness of life. For out of all time there comes to us less than what any one could call least, since "least" is at any rate some part; but this life of ours is next to nothing, and yet (fools that we are!), we marshal it in broad array!

These words I have written to you, not with the idea that you should expect a cure from me at such a late date—for it is clear to me that you have told yourself everything that you will read in my letter—but with the idea that I should rebuke you even for the slight delay during which you lapsed from your true self, and should encourage you for the future, to rouse your spirit against Fortune and to be on the watch for all her missiles, not as if they might possibly come, but as if they were bound to come. Farewell.

Basil to a Fallen Monk

This letter of rebuke to a monk appears only in later collections of Basil's letters, so that his authorship has been questioned by some. The author has cast the letter of rebuke into a classical Christian form. The rebuke is sharp and the recipient's sin taken as a very personal blow to the writer. The call for repentance is in a typical Christian form with an appeal to God's patience and mercy. The letter begins with the writer telling the monk that he cannot give the customary greeting because of the monk's impiety. It concludes with a solemn benediction and "amen" instead of the customary farewell.

In Letter 2, written to Gregory of Nazianzus, Basil gave the following advice:

Always avoid harshness, even when it is necessary to rebuke (*epitimēsai*) someone. For if you first lower yourself by showing genuine humility, then you will be well received by the one who needs your healing. The method of rebuke employed by the prophet is often useful to us. . . . [Nathan] used a fictitious character and made David the judge of his own sin.

Thus, in his letter to the fallen monk, Basil—like Paul (e.g., 1 Cor. 10:11) and Clement of Alexandria (*Instructor* 1.9)—looks to the scriptures for models of exhortation and rebuke just as the pagan rhetoricians and philosophers found them in Homer.

Cappadocia (?)   Fourth century C.E. (?)
Transl. by R. J. Deferrari, *Saint Basil: The Letters* 44 (LCL)

We say not, "Be it well with thee *(chairein),*" inasmuch as it cannot truly be well with those who are impious. For incredulity still holds me, and my mind cannot conceive of so great an iniquity and crime as you have committed, if indeed the truth of the matter is as it by this time appears to all the world. I wonder how such wisdom as yours was swallowed up, how such strictness became slack, how such blindness came to envelop you, how you were so utterly thoughtless as to work all this lamentable destruction of souls. For, if all is true, you have not only given your own soul over to the pit, but you have slackened the zeal of all who hear of this impiety. You have set aside the faith, you have missed the glorious fight. Therefore do I grieve for you. For what priest will not lament when he hears this? What ecclesiastic does not beat his breast? What layman is not downcast? What ascetic does not mourn? Mayhap, even the sun was darkened at your fall, and the stars of heaven tottered at your destruction. Even the unfeeling stones shed tears at your madness, and even your enemies wept because of your exceeding transgression.

Alas for your hardness of heart, your terrible cruelty! You feared not God, you were not ashamed before men, you paid no heed to your friends; but all alike you shipwrecked, of all alike you deprived yourself. Therefore again do I grieve for you, wretched man! You who proclaim to all your zeal for the kingdom fell from the kingdom. . . . You who instil fear of the doctrine in all men had no fear of God before your eyes. You who preach sanctity are found polluted. You who glory in poverty are caught stealing money. You who through your guidance set forth God's punishment have procured punishment for yourself. How shall I lament for you? How shall I grieve for

you? How did the early-rising Lucifer fall and meet destruction
upon earth? The two ears of everyone who hears thereof will
ring. How did the Nazarite who was brighter than gold become
blacker than coals? How did the honoured son of Sion become
an unclean vessel? Of him whose memory of the Holy Scriptures was noised about by all, the remembrance has this day
perished as soon as the ringing ceases. The man of quick intelligence has quickly perished. The man of a manifold mind has
committed a manifold sin. For they who have been aided by
your teaching have been injured by your destruction. Those
who gave ear to your discourses have stopped their ears at your
destruction. As for me, lamenting and downcast, utterly un-
done, eating ashes for bread, and having cast sackcloth over my
wound, I recount your praises in this fashion, or rather, as I
compose a funeral address for you, I remain disconsolate and
neglected; for consolation has been hidden from my eyes, and
I have no salve, no oil, no bandage to apply; for my wound is
painful. Wherewith shall I be healed?

Now if any hope of salvation still remains in you, any slight
recollection of God, any desire for the good things to come, any
fear of the punishments treasured up for the unrepentant,
come back to sobriety at once, lift your eyes to heaven, come
to your senses, cease your wickedness, shake off the drunkenness that has drenched you, rise up against that which has
overthrown you. Have the strength to rise from the ground.
Remember the Good Shepherd, that He will follow after you
and drive you into safety. . . .

There is still time for forbearance, time for long-suffering,
time for healing, time for reform. Have you slipped? Rise up.
Have you sinned? Cease. Do not stand in the way of sinners, but
leap aside. For when you turn back and weep, then you will be
saved. For out of labour cometh health, and out of sweat, salvation. Beware, therefore, lest, in your desire to keep agreements
with others, you transgress your agreements with God, which
you have confessed before many witnesses. Therefore do not
for any worldly considerations hesitate to come to me. For I
shall take up my dead and weep, I shall care for him, "I will
weep bitterly" "for the devastation of the daughter of my people." All are ready to receive you, all will aid you in your troubles. Do not lose heart; remember the days of old. There is
salvation, there is reform. Take courage, do not despair. There
is no law which condemns to death without compassion, but
there is grace which remits the punishment and accepts the

reform. Not yet closed are the gates; the bridegroom hears; sin does not prevail. Renew the contest; delay not; and have pity on yourself and on us all in Christ Jesus our Lord, to whom be the glory and the power, now and for ever, world without end. Amen.

Letters of Reproach *(oneidistikai)*

Reproach was a harsh blame that only the sternest sort of philosopher considered morally beneficial. I have included a brief discussion of reproach in order to illustrate the more extreme side of blame. Demetrius and Libanius agree that letters of reproach *(oneidistikai)* do not have a positive counter to their criticism. Demetrius writes:

> It is the reproachful type when we once more reproach, with accusations, someone whom we had earlier benefited, for what he has done.
>
> You were bound, after you had just come to know yourself, to behave peevishly toward others. But (even) now, although you are (still) being supported by us in the prime of your life, and owe your life to us, you think more highly (of yourself) than you should. We are to be blamed for this. For you were bound not to attain the character of a freeman. Even now you are not free, since you have acquired a servile character.

Libanius says:

> The reproachful style is that in which we reproach someone if he forgets how he has been benefited by us.
>
> The letter of reproach. You have received many favors from us, and I am exceedingly amazed that you remember none of them but speak badly of us. That is characteristic of a person with an ungrateful disposition. For the ungrateful forget noble men, and in addition they ill-treat their benefactors as enemies.

The letter of reproach, like the letter of blame, is most typically written by a wronged benefactor and concerns a failure of reciprocity. Unlike a "letter of blame" it involves a harsh criticism of the recipient's character. Both epistolary handbooks focus on the recipient's lack of gratitude. Demetrius blames the recipient for thinking too highly of himself (cf. Rom. 12:3) and accuses him of having a servile character. Libanius uses the expression, "I am amazed" (cf. Gal. 1:6), which is found in all kinds of blaming letters.

Letters of reproach seem to be absent from the corpus of early Christian letters. Paul contrasts the gentleness of his own teaching to harsher methods (1 Thess. 2:6–7) and the pastoral epistles polemicize against harsh and quarrelsome teachers (e.g., 2 Tim. 2:23–26).

Dio Chrysostom urges that the true philosopher will promote virtue and self-restraint "partly by persuading and exhorting, partly by abusing *(loidoroumenos)* and reproaching *(oneidizōn),* in the hope that he may thereby rescue somebody from folly and from low desires." Tradition made Diogenes into a master of abusing and reproaching. Letter 28 written by a Cynic in the name of Diogenes illustrates this picture of Diogenes.

Provenance unknown   Date unknown
Transl. by Benjamin Fiore, in *The Cynic*
   Epistles (ed. Malherbe), pp.121–125

Diogenes the Dog to the so-called Greeks, a plague on you! And this is already beginning to infect you, even if I should say nothing more. For although to all appearances you are men, you are apes at heart. You pretend to everything, but know nothing. Therefore, nature takes vengeance on you, for in contriving laws for yourselves you have allotted to yourselves the greatest and most pervasive delusion that issues from them, and you admit them as witnesses to your ingrained evil. Nor are you ever at peace, but you grow old in war your whole life long, evil persons fit for evil. You envy each other, when you see someone else who has a slightly finer mantle or a little more small change, or who has a more striking turn of phrase, or who had a better education. You decide nothing by sound reason, but you censure everything as you sink to what is likely and plausible and generally approved. You know nothing—as your ancestors did not, neither do you—but, being made a mockery of by your ignorance and senselessness, you become perverted, a fine way of acting! It is not only the Dog that hates you; nature itself does too. For little do you enjoy, but you are much distressed both before and after the wedding day, since indeed you were already spoiled and hard to please before you married. Look at the number and the quality of the men you killed! Some you killed in your greed during war, others in so-called peacetime, after hurling charges at them. Were not many hung on crosses, and did not many have their throats cut by the public executioner, while others drank a drug administered by the executioner, and some died on the rack? Of course, they seemed to be guilty! But, you blockheads, should one not attempt to educate such people rather than kill them? . . .

But this is not at all a matter of great consequence. Whenever you enact good things by force, one can see even superior things despoiled. And, you blockheads, whomever you lay your hands on, you wrong and chastise. And yet you yourselves deserve greater punishment. Whenever the so-called festival of Hermes or the Panathenaean games are held, both in the gymnasia and right in the market place, you eat and drink, get drunk, have intercourse, and act effeminately. Then you act profanely and, furthermore, do these things both in secret and in the open. The Dog cares nothing for these things, but you are anxious for them all.

And where you bar Cynics from a natural and true way of life, how would you not offend them? I, the Cynic, for my part punish you in word, but nature likewise punishes all of you in deed, for death, which you fear, dangles over you equally. Now I have often seen beggars enjoying health because of want, and rich people ailing from the intemperance of their unfortunate stomach and penis. For while you gratified these you were titillated for a short time by pleasure, which then displays great and grievous pains. . . . And should you regain your health, you have no thanks for the so-called doctors, but say that one must thank the gods. But if you do not, you blame the doctors. But I, at any rate, am more capable of gladness than sadness, and knowledge than ignorance. For I continued to talk with the wise Antisthenes, who carried on philosophical discourse only with those who knew him. He avoided the others who did not know nature, reason, and truth, and paid no attention to the childish beasts who do not understand the words of a Cynic, as is said in the letter. I call a plague on you real barbarians, until you learn in the Greek way and become true Greeks. For now those who are called barbarians are much more refined both in the place where they live and in their way of life. Those who are called Greeks war against the barbarians, while the barbarians think it necessary only to protect their own land, since they are content with what they have. But nothing is enough for you, for you are lovers of glory, irrational, and ineptly brought up.

Letters of Consolation *(paramythētikai)*

Consolation was very important in the Greco-Roman world. It had an important place in both the philosophical and the rhetorical traditions. Consolations took many forms: the consolatory speech of the rhetorical tradition, letters, elegiac poetry, dialogue, philosophical exhortation, and extended essay. Popular culture left its contribution to the tradition in myriads of epitaphs.

The original consolatory speech was considered to be the speech of Achilles to Priam in the *Iliad*. Rhetoric took this genre of exhortation into epideictic. Consolation was an important exercise in the elementary rhetorical exercises, *progymnasmata*. Menander Rhetor (413.5–414.30) divides the consolatory speech into two major parts, the lament and the consolation proper. The lament expresses grief over the death and treats the accomplishments and character of the person encomiastically. Menander advises that one follow the parts of the encomium—family, character, upbringing, education, accomplishments, actions—but not necessarily in the normal order. The consolation proper contains traditional materials such as quotations from the poets, examples, precepts, and arguments against excessive grieving.

There were many traditional arguments against grief. The following were the most common.

1. Death is inevitable.
2. Death is the fate of all, kings and beggars, rich and poor.
3. The person's memory and honor will live on in spite of death.
4. Death releases one from the evils of life.
5. The funeral and the tomb are a great honor to the deceased.
6. Either death is nonexistence and does not matter to the dead or it leads to some happier state of existence.

Giving consolation was considered one of the philosopher's chief functions. Dio complains that people generally wait until they are desperate before they approach a philosopher.

> The prosperous man . . . you would not easily find approaching these philosophers, or caring to listen to the teachings of philosophy. But if some disaster should overtake any one touching his livelihood, and he should become either poor after having been wealthy, or weak and powerless after having been influential, or should meet with some other misfortune, then he becomes much more friendly disposed toward that craft, somehow manages to endure the words of the philosophers, and practically admits that he needs comfort. And if it is his misfor-

tune to lose any of his relatives, either his wife, or a child, or a brother, he asks the philosopher to come and speak words of comfort, as if he thought it were only then necessary to consider how one may endure with resignation what happens and be able to face the future. (*Oration* 27.8–9)

Any kind of grief or misfortune might be the subject of the philosopher's consolation. Moralists adapted traditional arguments and hortatory materials to each person's situation. Cicero explains:

For there are definite words of comfort habitually used in dealing with poverty, definite words in dealing with a life spent without obtaining office and fame; there are distinctly definite forms of discourse dealing with exile, ruin of country, slavery, infirmity, blindness, every accident upon which the term disaster can be fixed. These subjects the Greeks divide up under separate heads of discourse, and deal with in separate books. (*Tusculan Disputations* 3.34.81)

Letters of consolation (*paramythētikai*) had a long and honored history in antiquity. Crantor (ca. 335–ca. 275 B.C.E.), a member of the Academy, has been called the creator of consolation as a literary form. His long letter to a certain Hippocles on the death of his children was much read, being used extensively in the consolations by Plutarch, Cicero, and Seneca. The Stoic Panaetius advised people to memorize Crantor's letter. Beginning with Crates, Cynics were known for their consolations. Epicurus wrote letters of consolation. Fragments of his letters to Hegesianax and to Metrodorus have survived. Letters of consolation were generally much shorter and more personal than consolatory speeches. Philosophers emphasized that the arguments of reason should subdue the feelings of grief. When moralists believed grief to be excessive their letters took the form of rebukes (e.g., Seneca, *Letter* 99; Ambrose, *Letter* 39). Occasionally both pagan and Christian writers followed the form of the consolatory speech or the funeral speech in more elaborate letters (e.g., Paulinus of Nola, *Letter* 13).

The letter of consolation was one of the most important types for Christian letter writers in the fourth and fifth centuries. They both used the traditional arguments and rhetorical methods and showed originality. Authors developed traditional commonplaces, such as, for instance, that life is a loan or that the virtues of the one who died ought to be imitated, in specifically Christian ways. The resurrection was typically the focus for arguments and laments that had the theme of hope. Several Christian writers also emphasized the humanness and reasonableness of genuine grief as long as it was not excessive. Some advice that Gregory of Nazianzus gave to a certain Timothy (*Letter* 164) became influential for Christian letters of consolation. Gregory says that philosophical arguments are to be reserved for the educated. The majority who lack culture ought to be given sympathy, encouraging exhortation, and often a rebuke for their lack of hope.

According to Demetrius:

> The consoling type is that written to people who are grieving because something unpleasant has happened to them. It is as follows:
>
>> When I heard of the terrible things that you met at the hands of thankless Fate, I felt the deepest grief, considering that what had happened had not happened to you more than to me. When I saw all the things that assail life, all that day long I cried over them. But then I considered that such things are the common lot of all, with nature establishing neither a particular time nor age in which one must suffer anything, but often confronting us secretly, awkwardly and undeservedly. Since I did not happen to be present to comfort you, I decided to do so by letter. Bear, then, what has happened as lightly as you can, and exhort yourself just as you would exhort someone else. For you know that reason will make it easier for you to be relieved of your grief with the passage of time.

The model letter deals with unspecified misfortunes but not death. The first part is a lament *(sympatheia)*. The writer feels grief and shares the recipient's grief. Next are the consolatory arguments proper, which are sometimes referred to as the *paraenesis,* the precepts against grief. The writer gives the argument from universal human suffering. After the epistolary commonplace that the letter is a substitute for the writer's actual presence, he exhorts the grieving person to have fortitude and grounds the appeal on two points: reason will control the grief and the passage of time will ease the burden.

The letter of consolation has the following fundamental elements.

1. The writer may have a wide range of positive relationships with the recipient.
2. The recipient has experienced some major misfortune that is apt to produce grief.
3. The writer expresses his grief and provides reasons why the recipient should bear up under the grief.

The New Testament

Like many complex paraenetic letters, 1 Thessalonians contains a consolatory section (4:13–18). This was recognized by educated Christian writers in antiquity (e.g., Theodoret on 1 Thessalonians; see *PG* 82, p. 648). Paul's call for the Thessalonians to stop grieving is a formulaic expression in consolatory literature. Like Paul, writers of consolations eased the sting of death by calling it sleep. The grieving were also told that the dead enjoyed safety and happiness with the gods. Furthermore, the deceased's survivors would someday join him or her. Letter writers also urged the grieving to take the words of consolation and use them to exhort themselves and others. Paul's attempt to comfort the grieving Thessalonians clearly follows ancient consolation to a point. His appeal to the resurrection and the return of Christ, however, introduces specifically Christian grounds of consolation that would be central to later Christian consolation.

Irene to Taonnophiris and Philo

Papyrus letters of consolation from Egypt are quite rare. When consolation does occur, it is often only a line in a letter devoted to other matters. In contrast, the great number of literarily transmitted letters of consolation are a reminder of the degree to which classical culture placed a person in a world quite different from that of the multitudes.

Irene's is a genuine letter of consolation. Taonnophiris and Philo are probably friends of Irene who have lost a son. Irene begins with a lament expressing her grief. She has grieved as much over the loss of their child as she did over the death of her own son. She seems to allude to attempts by her and her household to prevent the child's death by means of votive offerings to the gods. Then, Irene seeks to console her friends by suggesting the traditional sentiment that humans are helpless in the hands of fate. The implication is that the grieving should accept fate and carry on with their lives. She concludes with an exhortation for her friends to comfort one another, which is much like 1 Thessalonians 4:18.

Oxyrhynchus, Egypt   Second century c.e.
P.Oxy. 115
Transl. by author

Irene to Taonnophiris and Philo, take heart! I grieved and wept as much over the departed as for Didymas. I did every-

thing that was fitting, as did my entire household, Epaphroditus, Thermouthion, Philon, Apollonius, and Plantas.
But, for all that, there is nothing that can be done in the face
of such things. Therefore comfort one another. Farewell.

Sempronius to Satornila

Sempronius' letter to his mother is hardly a classical letter of
consolation. Nevertheless, it is typical of consolation in the papyri.
Sempronius informs his mother of the grief that his brother Maximus has been experiencing and asks her to console him. Then he
turns to offer a few words of consolation to Satornila herself.

Provenance unknown   Second century C.E.
Text ed. P. J. Sijpeseijn, *ZPE* 21(1976):
   179–180
Transl. by author

   Sempronius to his mother, greetings. As soon as you get this
letter let me know how you are getting along. For I am quite
anxious until I hear how you are doing. About my brother
Maximus I will now write to you so that you may console him
. . . lest out of grief he too might turn to something else. For
I know that you yourself also grieve for him, but, my lady, be
sensible because of my brothers. And this was fated because he
loved equally his daughters and sister Siborra. But what can we
do when God can do nothing? Farewell.

A Fragmentary Christian Letter of Consolation

This papyrus is of interest because it shows to what point Christian consolation had developed by the very end of antiquity. Although the writer's level of education is quite low, he or she knows
the Bible. Just as pagan literarily transmitted letters are often
steeped in the characters and language of the poets, so also this
letter is steeped in scripture.

Egypt   Sixth century C.E.
P.Oxy. 1874
Transl. by author

   You suffered like mother Eve, like Mary, and as God lives, my
master, neither righteous women nor sinners ever suffered
what you have suffered. And yet your sins are nothing. But let
us glorify God for he has given and he has taken away. But pray

that the Lord may grant them rest and consider you worthy to sing with them in Paradise when the souls of men are judged. For they have gone to the bosom of Abraham and of Isaac and of Jacob. But I exhort you, my Lord, not to let grief fall into your soul and ruin your life, but pray that the Lord may send you his blessing. For the Lord has many good things and gives cheer to those who are despondent, if they seek a blessing from him. And we hope in God that through this sorrow the Lord might send you joy and the lord your brother [. . .]

Phalaris to Lacritus

The following is one of the famous epistles of Phalaris shown to be pseudonymous by Richard Bentley in 1697–99. Written in the name of the tyrant of sixth-century B.C.E. Acragas in Sicily, it is actually a letter of consolation from the early Roman empire. Phalaris first shares his sympathy and then provides reasons to check excessive grief. His arguments are that Lacritus' son died fighting for his country and that he died a virtuous person.

Provenance unknown First or second century C.E. (?)
Text from Rudolph Hercher,
   Epistolographi Graeci, 410–411
Transl. by author

Your heavy sorrow at the death of your son is completely pardonable and I also deeply feel the loss as if the misfortune were my own. And yet I naturally act with greater firmness toward such things since I know that excessive sorrow is of no value. There should be much about your son that gives you consolation. First, he died bravely fighting for his country. Second, his death was made beautiful by victory. Third, he lived his portion of life without sin so that his peculiar virtue was sealed by death. For the good man may lose his virtuous character when he is alive. For fortune controls men more than judgment. He who dies without anything against him is consecrated with the most noble badge of glory. Think of him, therefore, as a child who has returned a noble gift for his birth and upbringing by his complete life of nobility and virtue. Reciprocate his gift by grieving for him mildly and moderately.

Gregory of Nazianzus to Gregory of Nyssa

Gregory of Nazianzus had been a friend of Basil's since their long years of philosophical and rhetorical schooling in Caesarea and Athens. When news of Basil's death reached him, he was in such poor health that he could not travel. He then wrote the following letter of consolation to Basil's brother and his own friend, Gregory of Nyssa. The consolation that follows Nazianzus' lament is a simple appeal for Gregory of Nyssa to rely on "philosophy." For platonizing Christians like the three Cappadocians, Christianity led to an ascetic and contemplative life that they called "philosophical." At its center was the ancient Greek belief that the task of the philosopher was to subdue the body and the emotions through reason.

Seleucia   January 379 C.E.
Text, *Gregor von Nazianz Briefe*,
   ed. P. Gallay
Transl. by author

It was reserved for my wretched life to learn about the death of Basil and the departure of that holy soul by which he left us in order to dwell with the Lord, after having made his entire life a preparation. And with the rest I am deprived of embracing his holy body and being with you who have the character of a philosopher and of consoling our common friends since my state of bodily health is precariously poor. For the sight of the emptiness of his church, sheared of such glory and bereft of such a crown is a thing which no reasonable person can behold with his eyes or comprehend with his ears. It seems to me that you have many friends and many words to console you but that no one can console you as you can yourself and his memory. You have become a model of philosophy for all others and like a spiritual standard both of discipline in prosperity and strength in distress; for philosophy knows two things, to act with moderation when things go well and with dignity when badly. That is our consolation to your Excellency. But for myself, who write these things, what time or words can console me except your fellowship and your company which the blessed one has left us in place of all others so that in you we might contemplate the image of him as if looking into a beautiful and transparent mirror?

Basil to Nectarius

Basil himself must be counted as one of the great writers of consolations in the early church. Stock themes and parts of the letter of consolation are present in Basil's letters but Christian themes, examples, and exhortations are also there. Basil typically relates how he heard of the death and then proceeds to the lamentation. If the occasion for consolation is death, he praises the deceased in a way reminiscent of the funeral speech. In Letter 5 he consoles a certain Nectarius, probably the future bishop of Constantinople, on the death of Nectarius' son. Basil also has appended a letter of consolation to his wife. He employs the following commonplaces: a call to reason, the hope of the resurrection, exhortation to courage, the incomprehensibleness of God's purposes, life as a loan, life as a journey, that all experience death, exhortation to emulate the deceased's virtue. Finally, in appealing to Job, Basil is using one of the most important Christian examples.

Provenance uncertain   Ca. 358 C.E.
Transl. R. J. Deferrari, *Saint Basil: The Letters* (LCL)

It was not yet the third or fourth day after I had been shocked by the news of your intolerable misfortune, and I was still in perplexity because the bearer of the distressing message was unable to tell clearly all that had happened, and so earnestly was I praying that it might not be true that I was reluctant to give ear to the common report, when I received a letter from the bishop which fully disclosed the sad tidings. How greatly I mourned thereat, and what tears I shed, why need I tell? For who is so stony of heart or so entirely without human feeling as to endure such a blow with complete indifference, or to experience in soul but a moderate grief?

The heir of an illustrious house, the bulwark of his race, the hope of his fatherland, the offspring of pious parents, a lad nurtured amid countless prayers, in the very flower of youth—he is gone, torn from the very arms of his parents. Is there a heart so adamant that such things would not melt and draw to a feeling of compassion? It is therefore no strange thing that your misfortune deeply touched us also, who from the beginning have been wholly attached to you, and have made your joys and griefs our very own. And yet hitherto at least it has always seemed that your griefs were few in number, and that for the most part your affairs ran smoothly with the stream; but suddenly, through the malice of the devil, all that happiness of home and that gladness of heart has been swept away, and our whole life has become a dismal tale. If, therefore, we would indulge in protestations and in tears because of what has happened, the span of our lives will not suffice; and though all mankind should mourn with us, they will not be able to match our sorrow with their lamentation; nay, even if the waters of the rivers should become tears, they would not suffice to satisfy our grief for what has happened.

If, however, we wish to make use of God's gift, which He has implanted within our hearts, we shall be comforted. By His gift I mean that sober reason, which knows how, both in fair weather to keep our souls within bounds, and, when the sky is more cloudy, to remind us of the lot of man, suggesting to us (what we have already both seen and heard) that life is full of such afflictions, that the examples of human misfortune are many, and above all, that it is God's command that those who put their trust in Christ shall not grieve for those who have been laid to rest, because of their hope of resurrection, and again, that for great endurance great crowns of glory await us at the hands of the Judge. If, then, we permit reason to whisper to us these reminders, perchance we shall find some slight relief from our trouble. Wherefore I exhort you, as a noble contestant, to stand firm against the blow, however great, and not to fall under the weight of your grief, nor yet to lose your courage, having assurance that even if the reasons for God's ordinances elude us, yet surely that which is ordained by Him who is wise and who loves us must be accepted, even if it be painful. For He Himself knows how He dispenses to each that which is best for him, and for what reason He sets for us unequal terms of life. For there exists a reason, incomprehensible to man, why some are sooner taken hence, while others are left behind to persevere for a longer time in this life of sorrows.

Therefore, above all, we ought to revere His loving-kindness and not repine, remembering that great and famous saying uttered by the great combatant Job when he saw his ten children in a brief moment of time slain at a single meal: "The Lord gave, and the Lord hath taken away: as it hath pleased the Lord, so is it done." Let us make these marvellous words our own; equal is the reward at the hands of the righteous Judge for those who exhibit equally noble deeds. We have not been bereft of the boy, but we have given him back to the lender; nor has his life been destroyed, but merely transformed for the better;

earth has not covered our beloved one, but heaven has received him. Let us abide a brief space, and we shall be with him whose loss we mourn. Nor will the period of separation be great, since in this life, as on a journey, we are all hastening to the same caravansary; and although one has already taken up his lodging there, and another has just arrived, and another is hastening thither, yet the same goal will receive us all. For even though your son has finished his journey first, nevertheless we shall all travel the same path, and the same hospice awaits us all. Only may God grant that we through virtue may become like to him in purity, that by the blamelessness of our character we may obtain the same repose as the children of Christ.

Additional Examples

Paraenetic Letters

For examples of simple exhortation in papyrus letters see Edgar and Hunt, *Select Papyri,* 101; *P.Oxy.* 744, 3057, 3069.

For non-Christian examples see Isocrates, *To Nicocles; Nicocles;* Pseudo-Isocrates, *To Demonicus;* Pseudo-Plato, *Letter* 10; for Epicurus the following fragments (Usener) are likely to have come from paraenetic letters: 97, 99, 105, 117, 130–131, 135, 181, 187, 200, 202–203, 207, 213–215; Cicero, *To Friends* 2.1, 4; 6.1, 10b; 10.1; 12.24; *To His Brother Quintus* 1.1; Pliny, *Letters* 2.6; 7.26; 8.13, 22, 24; 9.30; most of Seneca's letters to Lucilius are paraenetic; they form a narrative correspondence and should be read together; Crates, *Letters* 2–3, 9, 10, 15, 16–18, 19, 20, 28, 29, 31; Diogenes, *Letter* 3; Socrates, *Letters* 5, 6; Melissa, *Letter to Kleareta;* Theano, *Letter to Eubule.* For Christian examples see *1 Clement;* the letters of Ignatius; Polycarp, *To the Philippians;* Cyprian, *Letter* 6(81); Basil, *Letter* 2; Synesius, *Letter* 28; Augustine, *Letters* 19, 112, 210; Theodoret, *Letters* 77, 78, 132.

Letters of Advice

For examples of advising letters see: *P.Oxy.* 531; *P.Bon.* 1, 3, 4, 11, 12; Isocrates, *Letter* 1; Plato, *Letters* 6, 7, 8; Cicero, *To Friends* 15.4; cf. *To Atticus* 7.12; 8.3 (requests for advice); Pliny, *Letters* 1.23; 6.29; 7.9; Crates, *Letters* 12, 22, 25; Socratics, *Letter* 29; Fronto, *To Friends* 2.11; *1 Clement* (exhortation and advice); Augustine, *Letter* 228.

Protreptic Letters

Anacharsis, *Letter* 6; Crates, *Letters* 5, 6, 9, 13, 16; Ptolemy, *To Flora;* Basil, *Letter* 10; Augustine, *Letter* 218; Synesius, *Letter* 101 (cf. *Letter* 103); Gregory of Nazianzus, *Letters* 31, 178; Theodoret, *Letter* 76.

Letters of Admonition

P.Teb. I.23; *P.Oxy.* 938; Wilckens, *UPZ* 144; Cicero, *To Friends* 5.14; Diogenes, *Letter* 17; Crates, *Letter* 10, 26, 30, 32; Anacharsis, *Letter* 2; Socratics, *Letter* 34; Basil, *Letter* 261; Synesius, *Letter* 143.

Letters of Rebuke

ZPE 34(1979): 87–89 (= P. Michigan Inventory no. 339); Crates, *Letter* 26; Diogenes, *Letters* 28, 29, 32, 40; Socratics, *Letter* 8; Apollonius of Tyana, *Letters* 39, 51; Synesius, *Letter* 2; Augustine, *Letters* 247, 259, 262.

Letters of Reproach

P.Oxy. 2783; Crates, *Letter* 7; Diogenes, *Letter* 1; Synesius, *Letter* 121.

Letters of Consolation

P.Grenf. 2.36; *P.Wisc.* 84 (Letter 1); Cicero, *To Friends* 4.6; 5.16; Socratics, *Letter* 21; Seneca, *Letter* 99 (cf. *Letters* 93 and 98); Pliny, *Letter* 9.9 (cf. 1.12 and 3.21); Fronto, *On the Loss of His Grandson* 1, 2 (cf. *From Verus* 2.9); Phalaris, *Letter* 103; Plutarch, *Consolation to His Wife, Consolation to Apollonius;* Apollonius of Tyana, *Letters* 55, 58 (cf. 93 and 94); Julian, *Letter* 69; Libanius, *Letter* 344; Basil, *Letters* 6, 18, 26, 28, 29, 62, 101, 256, 257, 269, 300, 301, 302; Gregory of Nazianzus, *Letters* 167, 197, 238; John Chrysostom, *Letters* 71, 192, 197; Theodoret, *Letters* 7, 8, 12, 14, 15, 18, 27, 65, 69, and (in the Sakkelion collection) 12, 38, 132; Ambrose, *Letters* 15, 39; Augustine, *Letters* 92, 259, 263; *To Probus;* Jerome, *Letters* 23, 39, 60, 66, 75, 77, 79, 108, 118, 127; Paulinus of Nola, *Letter* 13; Sulpicius Severus, *Letter* 2.

11

Letters of Mediation

In letters of mediation one person makes a request to another person on behalf of a third party. These may be divided usefully but somewhat artificially into letters of introduction and other kinds of intercessory letters.

Letters of introduction *(systatikai)* are also called letters of recommendation. The recommended person is often the carrier of the letter so that the writer frequently envisages a face-to-face introduction upon the reading of the letter. The main purpose is sometimes to provide a person with credentials for some activity rather than merely to introduce the person. Egyptian papyrus letters of introduction are rather stereotyped and formulaic. This probably reflects the standard practice of popular professional letter writers who tended to set the local standards for writers with little education. Literarily transmitted letters of introduction are similar to the papyri but naturally show more variety and creativity since their authors usually had rhetorical educations.

Chan-Hie Kim has analyzed the formal parts of the Egyptian letters in great detail. He finds the following parts to the "typical" papyrus letter of recommendation:[11]

    I. Opening.
        A. Salutation, e.g., "Musonius to Nilus, greeting."
        B. Wish for well-being, e.g., "If you are well, we also are well."
   II. Background.
        A. Identification of the one recommended.
        B. Background proper, e.g., reason for the writer recommending the person.
  III. Request period.
        A. Request clause, e.g., "you would do well"; "you will be doing me a favor."
        B. Circumstantial clause, e.g., "if he has need of anything."

       C. Purpose and causal clauses, e.g., "so that you might introduce
           him to Tyrannus"; "for he is a trusted friend."
  IV. Appreciation (only in some papyri, but often in Latin letters), e.g.,
        "by doing this you will have my gratitude."
   V. Closing.
       A. Wish for well-being, e.g., "take care of yourself so that you
           might be in good health."
       B. Salutation, e.g., "farewell," "good luck."

In general structure if not actual phraseology, Demetrius and
Libanius' model letters resemble the papyri. Both suppose that the
person being introduced will also deliver the letter. Demetrius notes
that one praises the person to be recommended and tries to make
him personally known to the recipient. Libanius adds that the "letter of introduction" *(systatikē)* is also called the "entrusting letter"
(parathetikē). The latter term seems to have come into use only in the
first or second century C.E. The social basis for whatever transaction
occurs in the introduction/commendation is usually the positive
relationships the writer has with both parties. Typically he or she
appeals to both relationships in the letter. Thus Demetrius:

> The commendatory type, which we write on behalf of one per-
> son to another, mixing in praise, at the same time also speaking
> of those who had previously been unacquainted as though they
> were (now) acquainted. In the following manner:
>
> So-and-so, who is conveying this letter to you, has been
> tested by us and is loved on account of his trustworthiness. You
> will do well if you deem him worthy of hospitality both for my
> sake and his, and indeed for your own. For you will not be sorry
> if you entrust to him, in any matter you wish, either words or
> deeds of a confidential nature. Indeed, you, too, will praise him
> to others when you see how useful he can be in everything.

Similarly Libanius:

> The commending genre is that in which we commend someone
> to someone. It is also called the introductory genre.
>
> The letter of commendation. Receive this highly honored
> and much sought-after man, and do not hesitate to treat him
> hospitably, thus doing what behooves you and what pleases me.

We possess large numbers of Latin letters of introduction and
many Christian letters that have come to us through literary transmission. Both groups reflect regional and cultural variation but

share fundamental elements. The fundamental features of the letter of introduction are as follows:

1. The writer and the recipient share some positive relationship of reciprocity and are most often social peers in some respect (e.g., friends, family, government officials).
2. The writer intercedes on behalf of a third party in order to perform a favor for or through the third party and to establish a positive social relationship between the recipient and the third party.

In other letters of mediation the writer also intercedes on behalf of a third person but the purpose is not to introduce or necessarily to establish a relationship. Sometimes the purpose is to reestablish a broken relationship or to petition someone in authority on behalf of the third party. Many letters of supplication are extant in which the writer makes a request for mediation (e.g., *P.Lond.* 1976, 2045; *PSI* 972): e.g., a tenant may ask a landowner or patron to intercede and correct an injustice. In the fourth and fifth centuries there are letters from the sick and the anxious asking some holy man to intercede through prayers on their behalf (e.g., *P.Jews* 1925, 1926; *P.Herm.* 9; *P.Oxy.* 1494; *P.Heidelb.* 1.6). In the nonintroductory letters of mediation, the third party is very often in some kind of trouble and has sought the intercession of the writer.

The New Testament

Since travel and hospitality were extremely important in earliest Christianity, it is not surprising that letters of introduction are mentioned several times in the New Testament (Acts 9:2; 18:27; 1 Cor. 16:3; 2 Cor. 3:1–2). Philemon is an intercessory letter on behalf of the runaway slave Onesimus. Paul commends Onesimus on the basis of his Christian brotherhood with Philemon, the slave's master. He asks Philemon to accept Onesimus back as a brother "in the Lord" and "in the flesh." Philemon contains several phrases and topical and formal features of introductory and intercessory letters.

Many scholars once thought that Romans 16 was originally a separate letter of recommendation sent to Ephesus. Recent research has confirmed that the chapter belongs to Romans. In general practice, passages of recommendation in other types of letters or in "mixed letters" were not uncommon. Paul commends Phoebe, a "minister" and "patron" or "president" of a house church at Cenchreae, to the church at Rome (16:1–2). In Philippians 2:25–30

Paul commends the return of Epaphroditus and in 4:2–3 asks the community to support two women, Euodia and Syntyche. These commendations illustrate that recommendation did not always involve introduction. 1 Corinthians 16:15–16, 17–18; and 1 Thessalonians 5:12–13 have also been called passages of commendation, but exhortation also plays a role in these texts.

Kim has identified three parts to Paul's commendations: (1) An "introduction" that includes a petition and the phrase "concerning my child" in reference to the one being commended; (2) the "credentials," where Paul praises, or presents credentials, or, as in papyrus letters, recommends the person by describing the person's relationship to himself; (3) the "desired action," where Paul states what he wants the recipient to do.

Although Paul employs language and certain formal features that parallel the rather schematized papyrus letters, his freedom in writing introductions, commendations, and intercessions makes him better resemble the generally more educated writers of literarily transmitted letters.

The letter of 3 John also has typical features of letters of recommendation but displays freedom in composition in comparison with the papyri. It is a letter of recommendation on behalf of traveling brethren (vs. 8, 10) that also contains a short invective *(psegein)* in vs. 9–10 and exhortation in vs. 11–12.

Heracles to Musaeus

This letter is characteristic of Egyptian papyrus letters of introduction. Heracles writes in a way that envisages Dioscorus handing the letter to Musaeus. Notice the appeal to friendship.

Egypt   First century c.e.
Transl. by B. R. Rees, *P.Herm.* 1

Heracles to his dearest Musaeus, greetings. I request you to regard as introduced to you Dioscorus, who will deliver the letter to you; he is a very close friend of mine. By doing this, you will be conferring a favour on me. Farewell. Pharmuthi 13(?)

Apollonius to Sarapion

This letter is similar to Heracles' above, but Sarapion holds two important offices and the person being introduced is a member of the household rather than a friend. The letter ends with a version of a widely used pledge of reciprocity.

Egypt   6 C.E.
P.Merton 62
Transl. by author

Apollonius to Sarapion the strategus and gymnasiarch, many greetings and good health always. Isidorus, the one who is delivering this letter, is from my household. I ask you to consider him as introduced to you, and if he comes to you for anything do it for him for my sake. If you do this, I will be indebted to you. Whatever you wish to signify I will do without delay. Take care of yourself so that you will be in good health. Farewell.

Letter to a Tribune

Aurelius Archelaus wrote this Latin letter to a tribune of a Roman legion on behalf of a certain Theon. The name of Julius Domitius comes first because Aurelius Archelaus is his subordinate in the army. Compare this letter's "Look upon him as if he were myself" to Philemon 17.

Oxyrhynchus, Egypt   Second century C.E.
P.Oxy. 32
Transl. by author

To Julius Domitius, military tribune of the legion, from Aurelius Archelaus, his *beneficiarius,* greeting. I have recommended my friend Theon to you before, and now I ask you, lord, to look upon him as if he were myself. He is truly a man worthy of your love. He left his loved ones, property, and business to follow me and through it all he has seen to my safety. I ask you therefore to allow him into your company; he can tell you about our activities. Whatever he says about me is the truth. I have loved the man [. . .] may you and your household be happy and in good health, lord. When you read this letter imagine that I am speaking to you. Farewell.

A Letter to Sotas

The writer of this letter has employed Christian terminology known to us from several other papyrus letters. One of the two persons being introduced is a student of Genesis, probably a beginning catechumen.

Oxyrhynchus, Egypt   Fourth century C.E.
P.Oxy. 2785
Transl. by author

Rejoice in the Lord, beloved Papa Sotas, presbyter of Heracleopolis, we give many greetings. Welcome in peace our sister Taion who is coming to you and welcome for edification a man who is being taught about Genesis. Through these we and those who are with us greet our brothers with you. We pray for your health in the Lord, beloved Papa.

Leon to His Fellow Presbyters and Deacons

This letter also uses Christian terminology typical of the papyri. Note, however, how the letter ends with an "amen" and the unusual oath formula.

Oxyrhynchus, Egypt   Fourth century C.E.
P.Oxy. 1162
Transl. by author

Leon, presbyter, to the presbyters and deacons who serve together locally, beloved brothers in the Lord God, rejoice greatly. Receive in peace our brother Ammonius, who is coming to you. Through him we and those who are with us greet you and those who are with you kindly in the Lord. I pray for your health in the Lord God. Emmanuel is my witness! Amen!

A Recommendation to Paul

This Christian letter is one of a very few papyrus letters that aim at literary artistry. Paul and the recipient—probably Sarapion—seem to be church leaders. Paul writes Sarapion's name before his as a sign of respect. The first part of the letter is a proem that Paul has constructed around the motif and metaphor of the mirror. In accord with what the rhetoricians taught, Paul employs the proem to win the recipient's goodwill.

Oxyrhynchus, Egypt   Early fourth century C.E.
Ed. and transl. by E. G. Turner, *P.Oxy.*
2603, and J. H. Harrop, *JEA*
48(1962): 132–140

To my lord brother Sarapion Paul (wishes) well-doing. A man who has acquired a mirror or holds in his hand something else of that sort, in which faces are seen represented, has no need of one to tell him, or testify about the character that lies upon him, and his complexion, and his appearance, how it is. For he himself has become a witness by himself, and can speak about his own likeness. And when someone speaks to him, or explains about the beauty and comeliness about him, he does not then believe. For he is not like the rest who are in ignorance, and standing far from the mirror that displays the likeness of all. And it is the same with you my good friend. For as through a mirror you have seen my implanted affection and love for you ever fresh. Now concerning the acquaintances of ours who are bringing down the letter to you, there is no need for me to write, (knowing as I do) your friendship and affection to all, especially towards our brethren. Receive them therefore in love, as friends, for they are not catechumens but belong to the company of Ision and Nikolaos, and "if you do anything for them, you have done it for me." All the brethren here salute you. Greet also the brethren with you, both elect and catechumens. I pray you may be strong. And if you can write to the others about (them) don't hesitate, that they may receive them in each place.

Cicero to Publius Caesius

Cicero wrote numerous letters of introduction and intercession of varying length and intensity. The following example (*Letter* 13.76) is typical of his shorter letters of commendation.

Provenance uncertain   First century B.C.E.
Transl. by William Melmoth, revised by
author

To Publius Caesius. I most earnestly recommend to your favour my very intimate friend Publius Messienus, a Roman knight, who is distinguished by every valuable endowment. I entreat you, by the double ties of that love which I enjoy with you and your father, to protect him both in his fame and his fortunes. Be assured you will in this way win the affection of a man highly deserving of your friendship, as well as confer a most acceptable obligation upon myself. Farewell.

Pliny to Sabinianus

This letter of intercession on behalf of a freedman has often been compared to Paul's letter to Philemon.

Provenance unknown   Date uncertain
Transl. by William Melmoth, revised by
  author

Your freedman with whom you said you were angry has been with me; he threw himself at my feet and clung to me with as much submission as he could have done at yours. He earnestly requested me with many tears, and even with all the eloquence of silent sorrow, to intercede for him; in short, he convinced me by his whole behavior, that he sincerely repents of his fault. And I am persuaded he is thoroughly reformed, because he knows that he was wrong.

I know you are angry with him, and I know too, it is not without reason; but mercy is never more worthy of praise than when there is the justest cause for anger. You once loved this man, and, I hope, will again: in the meanwhile, let me only prevail with you to pardon him. If he should incur your displeasure hereafter, you will have so much the stronger a reason for your anger, as you show yourself willing to forgive him now. Allow something to his youth, to his tears, and to your own gentle disposition: do not make him uneasy any longer, and I will add too, do not make yourself so; for a man of your kindness of heart cannot be angry without feeling great uneasiness.

I am afraid that if I add my prayers to his, I would seem to be compelling you rather than asking you to forgive him. Yet I will do it and in the strongest terms since I have rebuked him very sharply and severely, warning him that I will never intercede for him again. Although it was proper to say this to him, in order to frighten him, it was not intended for your hearing. I may possibly have the occasion to again intercede for him and obtain your forgiveness if the error is one which is suitable for my intercession and your pardon.

Pliny to the Emperor Trajan

In Letter 10.5 Pliny requests Roman citizenship for an Egyptian physician from Alexandria and for two freedwomen on behalf of their mistress. Pliny had to write three further letters (10.6, 7, 10) about the physician because of legal complications.

Italy 98 or 99 C.E.
Transl. by William Melmoth, revised by
    author

Having been attacked last year by a severe and dangerous illness, I employed a physician whose care and diligence, Sir, I cannot sufficiently reward, but by your gracious assistance. I entreat you therefore to make him a citizen of Rome; for he is the freedman of one who is not a citizen. His name is Harpocras; his patroness (who has been dead a considerable time) was Thermuthis, the daughter of Theon. I further entreat you to bestow the full privileges of a Roman citizen upon Hedia and Antonia Harmeris, the freedwomen of Antonia Maximilla, a lady of high rank. It is at her desire I make this request.

Kaor to Abinnaeus

Kaor is the Papa of the small town Hermopolis. "Papa" was a title widely used for Christian leaders from monks to bishops of major cities ("pope" is derived from "Papa"). But Kaor is what we would call a village priest or pastor. He is a native Egyptian and his Greek is extremely poor. Kaor addressed his letter of supplication to Flavius Abinnaeus, a Christian prefect of the camp—a cavalry officer —at the town of Dionysias. Kaor's plea is that Abinnaeus pardon Paul, a deserter, "just this once."

Fayum, Egypt Ca. 346 C.E.
P.Lond. 417
Transl. by author

To my master and beloved brother Abinnaeus the Praepositus—Kaor, Papa of Hermopolis, greeting. I send many salutations to your children. I want you to know lord concerning Paul the soldier, concerning his desertion, pardon him just this once, since I don't have the time to come to you today. And again, if he doesn't stop, he will come into your hands another time. I pray for your long health my lord brother.

Synesius to His Brother, Euoptius

Bishops became mediators for the most varied social interactions and therefore wrote large numbers of introductory and intercessory letters. Augustine speaks of giving recommendations as a public duty to which he was bound if the appeal was legitimate (*Letter* 151.2). In his Letter 18 Synesius, bishop of Cyrene, writes a very matter-of-fact, everyday recommendation for an unnamed senator of Alexandria, who would be expected to introduce himself personally as he handed Euoptius the letter. Synesius gives his credentials —origins, connections of friendship, social status. Then he relates the occasion for the request and makes the request itself.

Cyrene   Ca. 399 C.E.
Transl. by Augustine Fitzgerald, *Letters of*
    Synesius

This man is a senator of the city in which my children were born to me. In some way or other we ought to honour all the people of Alexandria as fellow citizens and look upon them as such. What is more, he is a relation of that blessed Theodorus who is ever in our memories, and moreover he is by no means to be overlooked by such as hold the first rank in this city. These men have brought him to me with money for you to pay your troops. They have asked me to write a letter recommending him to your good graces, being assured that everything will go smoothly with him if he gets a letter of introduction from me to you and to a certain person. What they asked of me I have granted and if not in vain, it will be for you to make manifest.

Theodoret to Eustathius

The following (*Letter* 70) is one of several letters of recommendation that Theodoret wrote on behalf of refugees from the Vandal invasion of North Africa. In such cases educated writers aimed at producing sympathy for the person in question through pathetic narrative. The letter's recipient was Eustathius, bishop of Aegae on the coast of Cilicia in southern Asia Minor.

Syria   Ca. 440 C.E.
Transl. by Benjamin Jackson, *NPNF* 3

To Eustathius, bishop of Aegae. The story of the noble Mary is one fit for a tragic play. As she says herself, and as is attested by several others, she is a daughter of the right honourable

Eudaemon. In the catastrophe which has overtaken Libya she has fallen from her father's free estate, and has become a slave. Some merchants bought her from the barbarians, and have sold her to some of our countrymen. With her was sold a maiden who was once one of her own domestic servants so at one and the same time the galling yoke of slavery fell on the servant and the mistress. But the servant refused to ignore the difference between them, nor could she forget the old superiority: in their calamity she preserved her kindly feeling, and, after waiting upon their common masters, waited upon her who was reckoned her fellow slave, washed her feet, made her bed, and was mindful of other like offices. This became known to the purchasers. Then through all the town was noised abroad the free estate of the mistress and the servant's goodness. On these circumstances becoming known to the faithful soldiers who are quartered in our city (I was absent at the time) they paid the purchasers their price, and rescued the woman from slavery. After my return, on being informed of the deplorable circumstances, and the admirable intention of the soldiers, I invoked blessings on their heads, committed the noble damsel to the care of one of the respectable deacons, and ordered a sufficient provision to be made for her. Ten months had gone by when she heard that her father was still alive, and holding high office in the West, and she very naturally expressed a desire to return to him. It was reported that many messengers from the West are on the way to the fair which is now being held in your parts. She requested to be allowed to set out with a letter from me. Under these circumstances I have written this letter, begging your piety to take care of a noble girl, and charge some respectable person to communicate with mariners, pilots, and merchants, and commit her to the care of trusty men who may be able to restore her to her father. There is no doubt that those who, when all hope of recovery has been lost, bring the daughter to the father, will be abundantly rewarded.

Augustine to Fortunatus

Constantine's grant of the right of sanctuary to those who stayed within church enclosures only added to the public image of bishops as protectors of the innocent and oppressed. In Letter 115 Augustine deals with a case about which we know from three other letters (113, 114, 116). Augustine wants to protect the right of sanctuary and see that a tenant farmer receives a fair trial in spite of the fact that his opponent is a wealthy landowner. Fortunatus is bishop of Cirta.

Africa   Early fifth century C.E.
Transl. by Wilfred Parsons, *St. Augustine:*
   Letters

Augustine gives greeting in the Lord to the blessed lord, his revered and very dear brother and fellow priest, Fortunatus, and the brothers who are with you. Your Holiness is well acquainted with Faventius, who was a tenant-farmer on the estate of Paratianis. He had some kind of reason to fear the lord of the estate, so he took sanctuary in the church at Hippo, and waited there, as refugees generally do, to see if his difficulty could be settled by our intervention. Then, as often happens, he grew less and less careful as time went on and, as if his adversary had given up, went out to dinner with a friend, and was suddenly abducted, as he was coming out, by one Florentinus, said to be an officer of the count, and with him a band of armed men, as many as seemed necessary to them. When word of this was brought to me, and I still did not know where or by whom he had been carried off—although my suspicion fell on the man against whom he had taken refuge in the church —I sent at once to the tribune in charge of the coast guards. He sent soldiers; no one could be found. But by morning, we knew what house he was in, and that his captor had decamped with him after cockcrow. I also sent to the place where he was said to have been taken, but when the aforementioned officer had been found he would not allow the priest whom I had sent even to see him. On the next day I sent a letter requesting for Faventius the privilege which the emperor prescribed for such cases: namely, that those who were summoned to appear in court should be asked in a municipal session whether they were willing to spend thirty days under light guard, in that city, so as to set their affairs in order and provide for their expenses. My idea was that, during those days, we might perhaps settle his case by friendly discussion. But he had already gone off in the custody of that officer, and there is reason to fear that he may suffer some harm if he is brought before the governor's tribunal. Although the judge has the highest reputation for honesty, he has to deal with a very rich man. So, to prevent his money from influencing the court, I beg your Holiness, my beloved lord and revered brother, to be so kind as to take my letter to the honorable governor and read it to him, because I do not think it necessary to go into detail on the same case twice. Ask him to put off the hearing of the case, since I do not know whether he is guilty or innocent. And ask him not to make light of the fact that the laws were not observed in regard to the man, since he was carried off in that manner and not taken, as the emperor prescribed, to the municipal court to be asked whether he wished to take advantage of the postponement, and thus give us a chance to reach an agreement with his opponent.

Additional Letters of Mediation

Kim, *Letter of Recommendation,* pp. 150–238 (provides the Greek and Latin texts of 83 letters, mostly papyrus from Egypt); book 13 of Cicero's *Letters to Friends* (consists of letters of introduction and intercession); *P.Oxy.* 3129, 3149; 2 Kings 5:6; 2 Macc. 9:19–27; Aeschines, *Letter* 6; Demosthenes, *Letter* 5; Plato, *Letters* 13, 14, 15; Diogenes, *Letter* 48; Socrates, *Letters* 2, 3; Socratics, *Letters* 10, 25, 28, 30; Apollonius of Tyana, *Letter* 107; Pliny, *Letters* 2.9, 13, 15; 3.2; 4.4, 15; 6.8, 9; 7.31; 10.7, 104; Fronto, *To Friends* 1.1–10, 26; 2.4, 6; *To Marcus as Caesar* 5.49, 52; *From Verus* 2.7; Libanius, *Letters* 53, 100–296, 617–694, 1525; Basil, *Letter* 249; Gregory of Nyssa, *Letter* 8; Gregory of Nazianzus, *Letters* 21, 140; Synesius, *Letters* 2, 13, 38, 42, 59, 68, 83, 99, 117–119, 131, 135, 155; Augustine, *Letters* 41, 45, 96, 113–116, 139, 206; Jerome, *Letter* 103; Theodoret, *Letters* 29, 30, 31, 33, 35; Sidonius, *Letter* 2.5; Firmus, *Letter* 39.

12

Accusing, Apologetic, and Accounting Letters

Accusing *(katēgorikai)* and apologetic *(apologētikai)* letters were derived from forensic rhetoric. Modern students have often confused apologetic with accounting *(aitiologikai)* letters. Among extant letters there seem to be two basic classes of accusing and accounting letters. First are mostly papyrus letters that make charges or defenses by letter, usually in the form of petitions. These reflect common legal procedures but do not employ the technical methods of judicial rhetoric. Second are letters that make use of rhetorical practices of prosecution and defense speeches. The following fragmentary text illustrates the first sort of accusing letter, although for obvious reasons it lacks the names of those accused (compare Synesius' Letter 6 for an example from a well-educated writer).

Fayum, Egypt   Ca. 171 C.E.
Transl. by B. P. Grenfell and H. S.
   Hunt, *Fayum Towns,* 108

To Megalonymus, strategus of the divisions of Themistes and Polemo in the Arsinoite nome, from Pasion, son of Heraclides, from the Hellenion quarter, and Onesimus, son of Ammonius, from the Gymnasium quarter, both pig-merchants of the metropolis. Yesterday, which was the 19th of the present month Thoth, as we were returning from the village of Theadelphia in the division of Themistes, about dawn we were attacked halfway between Polydeucia and Theadelphia by thieves, who bound us and the guard of the watch-tower, and assaulted us with many blows, and wounded Pasion, and robbed us of a pig, and carried off Pasion's tunic [. . .], wherefore we present this petition and entreat you to register it, in order that when the culprits are discovered we may bring a charge against them on these counts, and [. . .]

The style of making or defending oneself against charges was also extended to personal relationships in friendly and familial letters. This is what Demetrius has in mind with his sample accusing letter. With letters like Demetrius', however, it becomes difficult to distinguish accusing from blame and accusing would seem to be blame with a forensic style.

> The accusing type is that which consists of an accusation of things that have been done beyond the bounds of propriety. For example:

> It was not pleasant for me to hear what was being said against me, for it was at variance with my upright conduct. On the other hand, you, too, conducted yourself badly when you placed yourself in the hands of the man who was speaking against me, even though you knew him to be a slanderer and liar. Speaking in general, you continue to cause (me) grief, for you have as friend someone whom you know to be an enemy of all men. Nor have you weighed this one fact, that the man who brings accusations against (absent) people while he is with you and others, is likely to do the same thing against you. Him, therefore, I blame because he does this, but you (I blame) because, although you seem to be intelligent, you nevertheless have no discrimination with regard to the friends you keep.

There has been much confusion about apologetic letters in modern scholarship. A "defensive tone" and self-justifications do not make an apologetic letter. Apologetic letters typically begin with an account of the charges made against the writer. If the letter does not begin with the charges, then they are alluded to or specifically stated in some other part of the letter. If someone has not made explicit charges, then a writer may anticipate charges and defend against those. Apologetic letters advance arguments against the charges. The forms of argument are often those of the *progymnasmata* or the rhetorical handbooks. Typically the arguments include a narrative of "what actually happened." These features are suggested in Demetrius' model letter (see the related types in Libanius, *Letters* 14, 19, 22, 61, 69).

> The apologetic type is that which adduces, with proof, arguments that contradict charges that are being made. For example:

> Fortune served me well by preserving for me important facts to be used in the demonstration of my case. For at the time that

they say I did this, I had already sailed for Alexandria, so that I happened neither to see nor meet the person about whom I am accused. Since there has been no disagreement between you and me, it is absurd for you to accuse someone who has wronged you in no way. But those who brought the accusation appear themselves to have perpetrated some foul deed, and, suspecting that I might write you something about them, they (took care) to slander me in anticipation. If you have believed their empty accusations, tell me. On the other hand, if you persevere with me as you should, you will learn everything when I arrive. In fact, one could be confident that, if I had at any time spoken against other people to you, I would also have spoken against you to others. So, wait for my arrival, and everything will be put to the proof, so that you may know how rightly you have judged me to be your friend, and I may prove you in deed. For I dare say that those who accused us will rather attack each other and choke themselves.

For the sake of space and since apologetic letters tend to be very lengthy, I will provide only some extracts from two apologetic letters.

Socrates' Letter 6

The sixth letter of Socrates is interesting because although it takes the form of an apologetic letter, its real function as a fictitious letter is to present Socrates as a model of the Cynic life. The unnamed recipient has made several charges against Socrates for his way of life. These "objections" are then taken up and answered one by one.

Provenance unknown   First century C.E. (?)
Transl. by Stanley K. Stowers in *The Cynic Epistles* (ed. Malherbe)

I have taken care of the two visitors, as you urged me to do, and I have sought out one of our companions who will plead their cause before the people. He said that he would serve quite readily because he, too, desires to please you. But concerning the money and the things you wrote about so mockingly, there is perhaps nothing unusual about some people inquiring, first of all, why I have chosen a life of poverty while others zealously pursue wealth, and then why, although it is possible for me to get large sums of money from many people, I willingly refuse gifts not only from living friends, but also from friends who have died and left gifts to me. And it is not surprising that other people consider one who is thus inclined to be insane. Yet one must consider not only this feature, but also the rest of our way of life, and if we appear different from others in regard to bodily practices, one must not be surprised if we also stand apart in our attitude toward material gain. Therefore, I am satisfied to have the plainest food and the same garment summer and winter, and I do not wear shoes at all, nor do I desire political fame except to the extent that it comes from being prudent and just. But those who pursue the luxurious life forego nothing in their diet, and they seek to wear different garments not only during the same year, but even in the same day, and they take great delight in forbidden pleasures. But concerning my children, and your statement that I should provide for them, all men can learn what I think about them. I consider the one origin of happiness to be right thinking. But he who has no understanding, but trusts in gold and silver, first thinks that he possesses the good which he does not have, and then becomes much more wretched than others. It is the same as if one person, although oppressed by poverty, will, even if not now, then certainly at some later time come to his senses, while another person, laboring under false notions of what it is to be truly happy, neglects what is truly beneficial, and being corrupted by affluence, in addition to the truly human goods which he has already failed to obtain, is defrauded of the hope of future good. For it is not possible for such a man to come safely to virtue, who is held captive by the flattery of men who are clever at speaking, and who is held captive by the sorcery of pleasures, which attack the soul through every sense organ and gradually drive out every bit of good or moderation.

Basil, Letter 8

Traditionally, Basil's Letter 8 has been understood as his defense to the Caesareans against charges that he deserted Caesarea for Nazianzus out of fear of the Arian party. The letter's authenticity has been doubted and it has been attributed to Evagoras. At any rate it clearly illustrates how arguments are marshaled against charges in an apologetic letter.

Nazianzus (?)   Fourth century C.E.
Transl. by R. J. Deferrari, *Saint Basil: The
Letters* (LCL)

I have often wondered what feelings you have conceived towards us, and for what reason you show such deference to our inferiority—paltry and insignificant as we are, and possessing, I suppose, no lovable quality—that you address us with words of exhortation, recalling our friendship and fatherland, as though you were endeavouring to induce, by an appeal to love of country, a runaway person to return to his home. That I have become a runaway I acknowledge, nor would I deny it; but the reason for this you may now learn, since you so desire.

In the first place, and chiefly, I was so confounded at the time by the unexpected event, as men are utterly and in a moment confounded by a sudden noise, that I could not control my reason, but, taking flight, removed myself to a distance, and I have sojourned a considerable time away from you; in the second place, a longing stole into my heart for the doctrine of God, and for the philosophy pertaining thereto. For how, I asked myself, could I overcome the evil that dwelt within me? Who would be a Laban to me, and free me from Esau, and lead me to the highest philosophy? But inasmuch as we have, with God's help, attained our goal as well as might be, having found a vessel of election and a deep well-spring—I mean Gregory, the mouthpiece of Christ—grant us, I beg, a brief space of time. We ask this not because we are fond of life in the cities—for we are very well aware that the Evil One devises deceit for men by such means—but because we consider the society of holy men most helpful. For by speaking now and then about the doctrine of God, and more frequently by listening, we are acquiring a habit of reflection that will not easily be lost again. Such is our present situation. . . .

In reply to those who slander us as being Tritheists, let it be said that we confess one God, not in number but in nature. For not everything that is called one in number is one in reality nor simple in its nature; but God is universally admitted to be simple and uncompounded. Yet God is not therefore one in number. What I mean is this. We say that the universe is one in number, but not that it is one in nature, nor yet that it is simple; for we divide it into the elements of which it is composed: fire, water, air, and earth.

The accounting type does not answer charges or necessarily even anticipate hostility but gives explanations for some sort of behavior that is open to misunderstanding or might be subject to blame. Demetrius writes:

It is the accounting type when we give the reasons why something has not taken place or will not take place. For example:

You wrote to me to come to you quickly, and I intended to do so. But all circumstances have been adverse to our taking ship. For of all the ships in public service, not a single one is available. And, even if we should find one, we are forced to do nothing about it, since the winds are against us. In the meantime, I have become involved in a lawsuit. Consequently, if all these things should change, expect me.

Anatolius to Sarapion

Anatolius belonged to a circle that worshiped Hermes Trismegistus. The letter explains why he was not able to travel to Sarapion and clarifies details about his subsequent plans.

Hermopolis (?)   Fourth century C.E.
Transl. by B. R. Rees, *P.Herm.* 2

To my master Sarapion, Anatolius, greetings. You know, my lord, that I pray both to see you in person and to speak to you, since you are my champion and among champions admirable. At all events, though often I was eager and ready for action, unavoidable reasons kept me from reaching you—on the one hand, the illnesses of my daughters (for it was one of the gods who in malice sent these upon me, and may he yet bring them to an end!), on the other the inexorable water of the cult of the god Hermes who protects. Therefore, in very truth, because my conscience is now sound and in keeping with your inexorable character, and because my lord brother Theophanes, our master, has made the journey up to me, in whom I have confidence . . . , everywhere . . . the worship of the sacred month of Pharmuthi having begun, in which many processions take place without stop and in due order, at which I must be present on two counts, by reason of the service due to the deity and because it offers the best opportunity for prayers for your health and good report. But I shall come, if the gods cooperate and make it possible, after the time of the worship in the month

Pharmuthi. May you enjoy everlasting happiness, my lord, and may the gods be with you, kindly disposed! *(Address)* To my master Sarapion, Anatolius.

Pliny to Paulinus

In Letter 9.37 Pliny explains to his intimate friend Paulinus why he will not be able to attend his installation as consul.

Tuscany   August 107 c.e.
Transl. by William Melmoth, revised by
    author

Pliny to his own Paulinus, greeting. As you are not of a disposition to expect from your friends the common ceremonies of the world, when they cannot observe them without inconvenience to themselves; so I too warmly love you to fear that you will misunderstand my behavior if I am not present with you on the first day of the month when you enter upon the consular office; especially as I am detained here by the necessity of letting my farms upon long leases. I am obliged to enter upon an entirely new method with my tenants. During the last five years, though I gave them large rent reductions, they have run greatly in arrears. For this reason several of them not only take no sort of care to lessen a debt which they have no hope of paying in full; but even seize and consume all the produce of the lands in the belief that it would now be no advantage to themselves to spare it.

I must therefore meet this increasing evil and find a remedy. The only one I can think of is, not to rent for money, but for a fixed share of the produce; and then to place some of my servants to oversee the tillage and the crops. And indeed, there is no sort of revenue more reasonable than what arises from the bounty of the soil, the seasons, and the climate. It is true, this method will require great integrity and diligent attention from the person I appoint as overseer, and put me to the expense of employing many hands. However, I must hazard the experiment; and, as in an inveterate distemper, try every change of remedy.

You see, it is not any pleasurable indulgence that prevents my attending you on the first day of your consulship. I shall celebrate it nevertheless, as much as if I were present, and pay my vows for you here, with all the warmest sentiments of joy and congratulation. Farewell.

The New Testament

There are no accusing, apologetic, or accounting letters in the New Testament, unless one considers the letters in Revelation 1–3 to be accusing letters. Paul plays with the idea of apology in 1 Corinthians 9:3–12 but the larger context of the chapter and the letter itself are hortatory. Second Corinthians contains accounting sections, e.g., 1:8–2:13; 7:5–16(?). Several sections in 2 Corinthians seem to be what might best be characterized as ironic apology, especially in chapters 10–12. Paul mentions charges in 10:10 (cf. 10:1).

Accusing and apologetic letters, together with letters of invective *(psektikai)*, played a very important role in the doctrinal controversies of the fourth and fifth centuries.

Notes

1. Transl. by David Worley in *The Cynic Epistles,* ed. by Abraham J. Malherbe (Missoula, Mont.: Scholars Press, 1977), p. 305.

2. On the social world of the early Roman empire, see John E. Stambaugh and David L. Balch, *The New Testament in Its Social Environment* (Library of Early Christianity; Philadelphia: Westminster Press, 1986).

3. *Seneca: Ad Lucilium Epistulae Morales,* ed. and transl. by Richard M. Gummere (LCL; Cambridge, Mass.: Harvard University Press, 1928, 1932).

4. *Papyri Bononienses,* ed. by Otto Montevecchi (Milan: Pubbl. dell' Univ. Cattolica del Sacro Cuore, n.s. 42, 1953), vol. 1. Transl. by Benjamin Fiore in Abraham J. Malherbe, "Ancient Epistolary Theorists," *(Ohio) Journal of Religious Studies* 5(1977): 43.

5. Synesius, *Letter* 101. The translation is my own.

6. My translation. The text and its interpretation is in some doubt: Rudolf Herzog, "Ein Menanderprolog," *Philologus* 89(1934): 185–196; Karl Gaiser, "Ein Lob Athens in Komödie," *Gymnasium* 75(1968): 193–219. My translation agrees with the consensus.

7. Transl. by Benjamin Fiore in Malherbe, ed., *The Cynic Epistles,* p. 95.

8. Transl. by Gummere (note 3 above).

9. Demetrius, *On Style* 227. Transl. by W. Rhys Roberts (LCL; rev. ed., Cambridge, Mass.: Harvard University Press, 1932).

10. I have modified Malherbe's translations of Demetrius and Libanius by using the translation "rebuke" for *epitimēsis* rather than "censure."

11. I have modified some of Kim's terminology.

Bibliography

Chapter 7: Letters of Friendship

On friendship see Horst Hutter, *Politics as Friendship* (Waterloo, Ontario: Wilfrid Laurier University Press, 1978), and the older but still valuable work by Ludwic Dugas, *L'Amitié antique d'après les moeurs populaires et les théories des philosophes* (Paris: Felix Alcon, 1894). On Roman friendship and letter writing see Friedrich Lossmann, *Cicero und Caesar im Jahre 54. Studien zur Theorie und Praxis der römischen Freundschaft* (Hermes Einzelschr. 17; Wiesbaden: Franz Steiner, 1962); and Erich Gruen, *The Hellenistic World and the Coming of Rome* (Berkeley: University of California Press, 1984), pp. 54–95. On philosophical friendship and the letter see Hildegard Cancik, *Untersuchungen zu Senecas Epistulae morales* (Spudasmata 18; Hildesheim: Georg Olms, 1967), pp. 46–113. On the friendly letter see Koskenniemi, *Studien zur Idee und Phraseologie des griechischen Briefes bis 400 n.Chr.* (Helsinki: Suomalainen Tiedeakatemia, 1956), esp. pp. 115–127; Klaus Thraede, *Grundzüge griechisch-römischer Brieftopik* (Zetemata 48; Munich: C. H. Beck, 1970). Thraede discusses the continuation of the friendly letter tradition by Christian writers in the first five centuries.

Chapter 8: Family Letters

On the Greek family see W. K. Lacey, *The Family in Classical Greece* (Ithaca, N.Y.: Cornell University Press, 1968); Claude Vatin, *Recherches sur le mariage et la condition de la femme mariée a l'époque hellénistique* (Paris: Boccard, 1970). On the situation in Egypt see Naphtali Lewis, *Life in Egypt Under Roman Rule* (Oxford: Clarendon Press, 1983). On family or household letters, principally papyrus letters from Egypt, see Aristide Calderini, "Pensiero e sentimento nelle lettere private greche dei papiri," *Studi Della Scuola Papirologica* 2.2–28; Maria Mondini, "Lettere femminili nei papiri greco-egizi," ibid., 29–50; Koskenniemi, *Studien*, pp. 104–114; Friedrich Joxe, "Le Christianisme et l'évolution des sentiments familiaux dans les lettres privées sur papyrus," *Acta Antiqua Academiae Scientiarum Hungaricae* 7.411–420; Giuseppe Tibiletti, *Le lettere private nei papiri greci del III e IV secolo d.C.: Tra paganesimo e cristianesimo* (SFL 15; Milan: Università Cattolica Milano, 1979).

For Christian and non-Christian papyrus family letters see *Select Papyri*, transl. A. S. Hunt and C. C. Edgar (Loeb Classical Library; London: Heinemann, 1932), pp. 269–394. Adolf Deissmann, *Light from the Ancient East* (London: Hodder & Stoughton, 1911), pp. 149–232, provides letters and discussions of their relevance to the New Testament.

Chapter 10: Letters of Exhortation and Advice

On exhortation and hortatory letters see Abraham J. Malherbe, *Moral Exhortation: A Greco-Roman Sourcebook* (Library of Early Christianity; Philadelphia: Westminster Press, 1986); "Exhortation in First Thessalonians," *Novum Testamentum* 25(1983): 238–256; Benjamin Fiore, *The Function of Personal Example in the Socratic and Pastoral Epistles* (Analecta Biblica 105; Rome: Biblical Institute Press, 1986); Rudolph Vetschera, *Zur griechischen Paraenese* (Smichow, 1912).

There is no good discussion of the protreptic tradition in English. The major work is the still-useful but conceptually problematic work by Paul Hartlich, *De Exhortationum a Graecis Romanisque Scriptarum Historia et Indole* (Leipziger Studien II, 1889). Also see the critical comments by Theodore Burgess in "Epideictic Literature," *University of Chicago Studies in Classical Philology* 3(1902). On protreptic in Christianity, see Giuseppe Lazzati, *L'Aristotele perduto e gli scrittori cristiani* (Milan: Società Editrice, 1938); Michele Pellegrino, *Studi sull'antica apologetica* (Rome: Edizioni di Storia e Letteratura, 1947); Stanley K. Stowers, *The Diatribe and Paul's Letter to the Romans* (Chico, Calif.: Scholars Press, 1981).

On consolation in general see Rudolph Kassel, *Untersuchungen zur griechischen und römischen Konsolationsliteratur* (Munich: C. H. Beck, 1958). On Christian consolation see Robert C. Gregg, *Consolation Philosophy* (Cambridge, Mass.: Philadelphia Patristic Foundation, 1975). On consolation in 1 Thessalonians see Abraham J. Malherbe, "Exhortation in 1 Thess.," *Novum Testamentum* 25 (1983): 254–256.

Chapter 11: Letters of Mediation

Clinton Keyes, "The Greek Letter of Introduction," *AJPh* 56(1935): 28–44; Chan-Hie Kim, *Form and Structure of the Familiar Greek Letter of Recommendation* (Society of Biblical Literature Dissertation Series 4; Missoula, Mont.: Scholars Press, 1972); Hannah Cotton, "Greek and Latin Epistolary Formulae: Some Light on Cicero's Letter Writing," *AJPh* 105(1984): 409–425. All three of these write about the letter of introduction. Kim and Cotton successively build upon and correct their predecessors. For a less personal relative of the intercessory letter see John L. White, *The Form and Structure of the Official Petition* (Society of Biblical Literature Dissertation Series 5; Missoula, Mont.: Scholars Press, 1972).

Chapter 12: Accusing, Apologetic, and Accounting Letters

On apologetic letters see Jonathan Goldstein, *The Letters of Demosthenes* (New York: Columbia University Press, 1968), pp. 99–184; Arnaldo Momigliano, *The Development of Greek Biography* (Cambridge, Mass.: Harvard University Press, 1971); H. D. Betz, *Galatians: A Commentary on Paul's Letter to the Churches in Galatia* (Philadelphia: Fortress Press, 1979), esp. pp. 14–24. See the argument against Betz's view of Galatians as an apologetic letter by George Kennedy in *New Testament Interpretation Through Rhetorical Criticism* (Chapel Hill, N.C.: University of North Carolina Press, 1984), pp. 144–152.

Index of Names

Index of Selected Epistolary Commonplaces

Index of New Testament References